JAMIE DORNAN

SHADES OF DESIRE

JAMIE DORNAN

SHADES OF DESIRE

ALICE MONTGOMERY

MICHAEL JOSEPH
an imprint of
PENGUIN BOOKS

MICHAEL JOSEPH

UK | USA | Canada | Ireland | Australia
India | New Zealand | South Africa

Michael Joseph is part of the Penguin Random House group of companies
whose addresses can be found at global.penguinrandomhouse.com.

First published 2015
001

Copyright © Alice Montgomery, 2015

For picture credits see page 250

The moral right of the author has been asserted

Set in 13/16 pt Minion Pro
Typeset by Jouve (UK), Milton Keynes
Printed in Great Britain by Clays Ltd, St Ives plc

A CIP catalogue record for this book is available from the British Library

ISBN: 978–0–718–18012–6

www.greenpenguin.co.uk

MIX
Paper from
responsible sources
FSC® C018179

Penguin Random House is committed to a
sustainable future for our business, our readers
and our planet. This book is made from Forest
Stewardship Council® certified paper.

Contents

1

The Hunt Is On

Summer 2013, and the hunt was on to find the actor who would play one of the most talked about and hotly anticipated film roles in years. Some years previously, a totally unknown author by the name of E L James had self-published a book that very quickly turned into a *succès de scandale*. This book had gathered momentum until it was picked up by a mainstream publisher, and the result, *Fifty Shades of Grey*, turned into an international sensation. The tale of the darkly brooding Christian Grey and the innocent yet knowing Anastasia Steele quickly became a phenomenon, topping bestseller lists all over the world, making a film of the novel a near certainty. But who would end up playing the lead?

There was certainly no shortage of speculation, with half of Hollywood's young A list being name-checked constantly. Ryan Gosling's name had come up, along with Matt Bomer, William Levy, Channing Tatum, Alexander Skarsgård, Stephen Amell, Ian Somerhalder and Michael Fassbender, some of this speculation more serious than others. Some of the actors involved admitted they had been approached about the role, although in the event, the final casting surprised everyone. Ian Somerhalder, who certainly had the looks, lobbied quite publicly for the part, tweeting about how much he'd love to play it, although in the end it was not to be. In other cases, such as that of Matt Bomer, it was the fans that took to Twitter, running a campaign for him to win the role.

Perhaps inevitably, Robert Pattinson's name had been bandied about – he, after all, was the heartthrob star of the *Twilight* series, playing the world's most attractive vampire in the shape of Edward Cullen, and it was *Twilight* that had inspired the early version of *Fifty Shades*, which had actually started out as a piece of fan fiction. Rumours that he was involved were quashed pretty quickly, though, not least because Pattinson was said to have been offered the role but had decided against taking it after listening to the advice of his *Twilight* co-star and then girlfriend Kristen Stewart. She had told him he would never break free from the part, and she was almost certainly right.

And so the search went on. This was not something to be taken lightly: given the phenomenal success of the books, the films were certain to be blockbusters, generating hundreds of millions of pounds in revenue and very possibly more. But taking the part was a double-edged sword. Whoever took it on had to get it right: the story revolved around a sadomasochistic relationship, after all, and it would be too easy to put in an over-the-top performance and turn the film into a laughing stock. There were all kinds of different issues at play: would an already established actor risk his reputation on such a tricky project? Was there too much at stake to cast a complete unknown? The search – and the speculation – went even further into overdrive.

And then, finally, came an announcement: a British actor was to take the role. Charlie Hunnam, a handsome young man best known for his work in *Sons of Anarchy*, in which he played Jackson 'Jax' Teller, had first come to the attention of the public when he played Nathan Maloney in the Channel 4 series *Queer as Folk*. He had also appeared in the films *Green Street Hooligans*, *Children of Men* and *Pacific Rim*, and at thirty-three he was just the right age for the role. E L James appeared to be delighted: 'The gorgeous and talented Charlie Hunnam will be Christian Grey,' she tweeted. It was a compromise in the best possible way – Charlie was a known quantity, but not an A-lister with too much at stake, so he could take a risk. But was E L James as pleased as she made out? The writer Bret Easton Ellis, who, it was rumoured, had wanted to pen the script for the film, tweeted that in reality James had been hoping Pattinson would get the role. After all, her initial take on Christian was made with Rob in mind. 'E L James and I were at Rob Pattinson's house when she admitted that Rob was the first choice for Christian,' he tweeted. 'Ian Somerhalder never in running. Matt Bomer was never in the running. When E L James asked me who I thought should be Christian I said, "James Dean, of course," and then she shoved me. We were both very wasted.'

As ever, Twitter lit up at the news, with fellow stars flocking to pledge their support. 'I don't think I've worked with a harder working or more humble actor than Charlie Hunnam, he will be great as Christian Grey,' tweeted *True Blood* star Robert Kazinsky. 'Congrats to Charlie Hunnam on the *Fifty Shades of Grey* role. It was a tough fight but the actor with the longer hair won. #bummed,' was *Office* actor Rainn Wilson's take. 'I lost the role in *Fifty Shades of Grey* so you won't be hearing from me for a while,' chipped in *Girls* star Lena Dunham, although whether this was serious was a moot point and anyway, she would hardly have been going up against Charlie for the role.

Everyone was happy. Charlie certainly seemed to be pretty pleased about it and was looking forward to co-starring with Dakota Johnson, the actress daughter of Don Johnson and Melanie Griffith, who had been cast as Anastasia Steele. 'As soon as we got in the room and I started reading with Dakota, I knew that I definitely wanted to do it, because there was a tangible chemistry between us,' he said in an interview with the *Hollywood Reporter*. 'It felt kind of exciting and fun and weird and compelling, and so that was it.'

The blogosphere, however, erupted, claiming that Hunnam and his co-star Dakota were not physically right for the roles. Indeed, feelings ran so high that some fans even started a petition on *Change.org* to replace the pair. This in itself wasn't unusual – the casting in high-profile films often causes rows, with the author Ian Fleming famously disapproving of the casting of Sean Connery in the role of James Bond. More recently Robert Pattinson had had to endure a great deal of umbrage from fans when he was cast as Edward Cullen, until

Twilight author Stephenie Meyer stepped in and said he was her first choice for the role. The controversy, while a little bruising, should have been no surprise, and at any rate there were plenty of Hunnam admirers who asserted that while he might not look exactly like the books' description of Christian Grey, his charisma and sex appeal more than made up for it. Even his girlfriend Morgana McNelis was dragged into it, with Charlie admitting it wouldn't be easy for her: 'She's required to share parts of me that she wouldn't really want to share, so of course, with the nature of this role that's going to be times ten,' he told *Hollywoodlife.com*. 'But she loved the books, she read them and she was really excited at the potential of this opportunity for me. If anything, I think it will bring us closer.' At least it was clear that he was taking the role seriously.

For reasons that were never entirely made clear, however, in October 2013, Hunnam announced that he was stepping down from the role. The rumour mill went into overdrive: was it because of artistic differences with the director? A shoddy script? Or had the pressure just got too much for him, making him think he couldn't live up to the hype? Possibly wisely, Hunnam kept schtum on the subject, and when he did break his silence, at an appearance at the annual Hogs for Heart event benefitting One Heart Source education programmes in Africa, he didn't shed a great deal of light on what had happened. 'I'm good,' he assured reporters. 'I am just really concentrating on work. It's been a really busy time.'

Universal Pictures released a statement, which the

Hollywood Reporter published. 'The filmmakers of *Fifty Shades of Grey* and Charlie Hunnam have agreed to find another male lead given Hunnam's immersive TV schedule, which is not allowing him time to adequately prepare for the role of Christian Grey,' it said. This wasn't very informative either, and no one seemed to know exactly what had gone wrong.

It emerged that Hunnam's father had passed away the previous May, and there was speculation that might have had something to do with it. He was also nearing the end of filming *Sons of Anarchy*. 'I have had some family stuff going on, so just trying to stay focused and stay positive and keep trying to do a good job at work and be with my family and stay positive,' he told a reporter on *E! News*. 'Like I said, I've got some family stuff I have to tend to. So when I wrap the show, I am going to go to England and see my people and then I have a film that I am doing with Guillermo [del Toro]. So I am going to go and do that and concentrate on the final seasons of *Sons*.' More than that he would not say, although there was further speculation that he could not face becoming the subject of fan hysteria in the way that, say, Robert Pattinson had done. In Pattinson's case, fans had once even put him in physical danger, having inadvertently pushed him into the path of an oncoming taxi. Hunnam had already achieved a degree of recognition and success, but the role of Christian was bound to put him in a different league altogether, and that level of stardom isn't for everyone. '[Two] sources now say Hunnam got cold feet on the [*Fifty Shades*] movie, TV schedule said to have nothing to do with his exit,' Matt Belloni, executive editor on the *Hollywood Reporter*, said on Twitter.

An unnamed source spoke to *People* magazine. 'He dropped out of the project because he didn't want to be typecast,' he said. 'He didn't want the Robert Pattinson-esque attention that would come along with taking on this role.'

But according to others, another quite spectacular and almost career-ending disaster nearly two decades earlier was what really weighed on Charlie's mind. In 1995 the director Paul Verhoeven was responsible for a film called *Showgirls* about an ingenue who rises from stripper to show girl in the seedy venues of Las Vegas. It was a film that was so uniquely awful it became famous as an example of how *not* to make a film (although in all fairness, it did very well in the home video market, as it then was, and went on to establish itself as a sort of cult success.) The star was a woman called Elizabeth Berkley, who had been a teen actress, making her name in the series *Saved By the Bell*, playing a character called Jessie Spano in the late 1980s and early 1990s. Due to the very adult nature of *Showgirls*, the film was meant to be her breakthrough role into the world of mainstream filmmaking, but such was the derision with which the film was greeted, it all but brought her career to a full stop. Elizabeth does still work as an actress, but at nothing like the level she was once predicted to, and the reason seems to be that ill-fated starring role.

There were rumours that Hunnam feared the same thing

might happen to him. 'Charlie got cold feet,' a source told *HollywoodLife.com*. 'He wanted to get out of the movie because he was feeling like it would be his version of *Showgirls* and he didn't want to be remembered for that.' This was, it should be said, unlikely. The director of *Fifty Shades* was the acclaimed artist Sam Taylor-Johnson, a totally different creature from the outrageous Verhoeven, and it was a certainty from the outset that she had no intention of allowing her film to become a laughing stock.

That didn't stop the rumour mill, though. Had he suffered a lack of nerve because of the intensely controversial nature of the role, or were other factors to blame. 'What he was taking on with this role was not what Charlie wants in his future career,' an insider was reported as saying on *E! News*. 'The attention and the pressure was intense. More than anything, he hates attention, and being in *Fifty Shades of Grey* would force him to do lots of media . . . Charlie doesn't want to be massively famous.'

And if you didn't want to be famous, this really wasn't a project to be involved with. E L James was philosophical, saying, 'I wish Charlie all the best.'

And so it was back to square one. The hunt was on again and names were bandied about all over the place, including some who had previously been thought to be in the running: Alexander Skarsgård of *True Blood*, Christian Cooke of *Romeo and Juliet*, Theo James of *Divergent* and Alex Pettyfer of *I Am Number Four* were all said to be in with a shot. It was now that the Twitter campaign to get Matt Bomer the role really sprang into action, and the fans made no bones about making their wishes clear. Some of the messages, many somewhat grammatically challenged, ran as follows: 'Yes yes yes Charlie Hunnam is not going to be Christian Grey anymore! PICK MATT BOMER!!!', 'Please, please, please give Matt Bomer the role as Christian Grey in *Fifty Shades of Grey*!', 'RT IF YOU WANT MATT BOMER AS CHRISTIAN GREY', 'I wish Matt Bomer would be castes as Christian Grey', 'if they would've just listened to the internet and casted Matt Bomer from the start.', 'MATT BOMER PLEASE!!! Fifty shades baby!!!', 'Can Matt Bomer please be Christian Grey?!', 'Matt Bomer is my choice to play Christian Grey!' And so it went on. Online multiple-choice questionnaires even went up: did the fans want Ian, Matt or Alex?

The hard-hearted bosses in Hollywood weren't listening, though. Even in these egalitarian days, when so much of life is dictated by Twitter, there was too much riding on this film to listen to the fans. They had to be certain that whoever was chosen for the role would set the screen ablaze. 'There is a lot that goes into casting that isn't just looks', producer Dana Brunetti had tweeted the previous September. 'Talent, availability, their desire to do it, chemistry with the other actor, etc. So if your favourite wasn't cast, then it is most likely due to something on that list. Keep that in mind while hating and keep perspective.' It was a slightly exasperated remark but then again, in the days before Twitter, Hollywood could cast its films without interference and comment from the rest of the world.

There was a renewed call for Robert Pattinson to take the role, and this time round the argument was not that he would be trapped in the role of Edward/Christian for ever, but rather that playing damaged Christian, with his penchant for bondage and S&M, would be a way of stepping away from Edward, who is possibly the most clean-living and pure-hearted vampire to have ever flown by night. Pattinson refused to play ball, though. There had been some talk that Hunnam had beaten him to the role, but the reality was that Pattinson didn't think it was a good idea, and he was probably right. Now separated from Kristen, it was time for a change. 'Rob is not going to change his mind about doing the film, he doesn't want to commit to multiple films and another franchise,' a source told *HollywoodLife.com* (apart from the *Twilight* films, Pattinson had also starred in *Harry Potter* as Cedric Diggory, the Hufflepuff prefect). 'He wants his career to go in a completely different route. Add that to the fact that he is not the number-one pick from the producers, it's just not happening.'

It was now that another name cropped up, that of Jamie Dornan, a British model and actor. Insiders said he was a strong contender for the role. He certainly looked the part, and in many ways he fulfilled the same criteria as Hunnam – he was a known quantity, but not too well-known. As well as proving beyond a shadow of a doubt that he was photogenic on the back of several modelling campaigns, he was beginning to build a reputation as an up-and-coming actor. Could the film-makers finally have found their Christian Grey?

One person who was having a big say in the casting was Dakota. It was imperative that the right chemistry existed between the two leads, and given that she was to play Anastasia, she took a very active interest in who would become her co-star, working with the producers in choosing who would play the role. 'She's just so Anastasia Steele,' Michael De Luca, one of the producers, told *E! News*. 'She's the best partner a producer could have.' She was 'helping us look through the candidates to see which chemistry kind of catches our attention'.

Strangely enough, this was not without precedent: a similar situation existed when casting the *Twilight* film. Kristen Stewart had been cast as Bella Swan before Edward had been chosen, and the director Catherine Hardwicke was equally intent that the requisite chemistry should exist between the two leads, so Kristen was given a say in who would star alongside her. When Robert Pattinson's name came up, it was by no means a done deal, and Catherine's solution was to spend some time with just the two of them and a camera to see how they interacted together. The rest is showbiz history, and the chemistry was such that eventually they became a real-life couple. It seemed appropriate that the film of a book that had been inspired by *Twilight* should be cast in the self same way.

The behind-the-scene manoeuvres continued, but as autumn progressed, it looked increasingly likely that the producers had finally found their man. The *Hollywood Reporter* certainly thought so. In October 2013, it reported that Jamie had got the role, and on 23 October came the announcement everyone was waiting for when *Variety* reported that Jamie had indeed got the part.

'Northern Irish actor Jamie Dornan has been tapped to replace Charlie Hunnam as Christian Grey in the Universal and Focus adaptation of *Fifty Shades of Grey*,' it said. 'The project was hit with a huge curveball when Hunnam departed after being attached for just a month. Universal said Hunnam's exit was due to scheduling issues with *Sons of Anarchy* and upcoming movie *Crimson Peak*, but some sources said battles over a rewrite and the actor's doubts about the role may have played a part in his decision. When Hunnam exited, U and Focus execs decided to go for more of a discovery and brought in Dornan and Billy Magnussen to test with Johnson last Friday. Though the studio considered bringing in more actors to test, as of Wednesday morning sources said no one else had been brought in.' *Variety* also commented on the fact that Jamie had previously been an underwear model, which might come in useful as 'the part will require him to act in explicitly sexual scenes'. Attention now focused on the rest of the casting, but everyone could relax (in as much as anyone can relax in Hollywood) now that the two central roles had been cast.

It was a match: the all-important chemistry with Dakota was there. 'Jamie *is* Christian and has a thousand times more chemistry than she had with Charlie, and she had chemistry with Charlie,' a source told *HollywoodLife.com*. 'Everyone is very, very happy with the results.' That included Dakota, who was heavily involved in the casting. 'Dakota was in constant contact with the producers and the studio and was very willing to help out in any way,' said the source. 'She was extremely hands on, no pun intended. Dakota had a pretty amazing read with Jamie.' It was good news for everyone involved, but it was also building up expectations. The pressure was on and filming hadn't even begun.

Fellow celebs leapt into action on Twitter: 'I've had a crush on Jamie Dornan for a decade!' – Elizabeth Banks. 'I'm a monstrous @JamieDornan1 fan. Wasn't allowed to be attracted to him on *The Fall* bc he played a sexmurderer. *Fifty Shades* is my big chance!' – Lena Durham. 'Wait, Christian Grey isn't a murderer right?' – Lena Durham. 'JamieDornan1 is my Mr Grey #FiftyShadesOfDornan' – Josh Dallas. 'RT if you are excited for the "50 Shades of Grey" movie starring @JamieDornan1! #JamieDornan #can't wait' – Crystal Hefner. '@ochocinco: I didn't get the role for Christian Grey. RT @_RLD: Ummm Christian Grey was Caucasian. @ochocinco: They could've bleached me for the movie' – Chad Johnson. 'I think that Jamie Dornan is the perfect choice to play Christian Grey in *FIFTY SHADES OF GREY*. Smartest casting decision in a long time' – Bret Easton Ellis; the author was evidently keeping a very close eye on all things Christian Grey.

The fans were happy, too, albeit in moderation. The general consensus was that Jamie was a better choice than Charlie, although quite a few still felt the need to declare their preference for Matt. He had never seriously been in the running, though, even after Charlie dropped out; the only real contenders were Jamie and Alexander Skarsgård.

Meanwhile, online sites began feverishly comparing the relative charms of Jamie and Charlie, and bare-chested pictures of the two of them began to appear everywhere. Both looked pretty good, but the spotlight focused on Jamie now.

As the world began to digest the momentous news, however, the rumour mill started up again. It was whispered that Jamie might have been approached while Charlie was still signed up to do the film, which put a very different perspective on things. A few other actors, including Billy Magnussen and François Arnaud, were said to have been tested too. It was whispered that Charlie had only been due to receive a sum in the low six figures for his work on the film, a tiny amount compared to the millions that are regularly paid for starring roles. Meanwhile, it emerged that a new screenwriter, Patrick Marber, had been engaged to polish up the script, giving rise to further suspicions that the original had not been entirely up to scratch.

Despite the rumours, the announcement of Jamie's casting breathed new vigour into the project and sparked a wave of excitement about one of the most hotly anticipated films in years. As pictures of Jamie in his underpants continued to spread across the net, the consensus was that the producers had got it right: for a start, he certainly looked the part.

There was an increasing amount of curiosity about the man who was about to become the focal point of a huge amount of publicity. It was known that he'd acted before, that he came from Northern Ireland, that he'd once dated Keira Knightley and that he looked pretty good in his underwear, but other than that Jamie remained something of an unknown quantity, enigmatic even, just like Christian Grey. Could he set the screen alight and project the tormented soul of Christian? And just who was this man who had beaten off the stiffest competition in hot young Hollywood to take on a role that was bound to make him into a major international star?

2

Wee Baby Jamie

It was 1 May 1982, and in County Down, Northern Ireland, James C. Dornan, always known as Jim, and his wife Lorna, were wildly excited. They had just welcomed their third and youngest child into the world, another James, always to be known as Jamie. Two girls, Liesa and Jessica, had already arrived, without the help of their father Jim, who was an obstetrician and a gynaecologist, but who was not, due to the mores at the time, allowed to help at the births of his own children. Indeed, he was even required to leave the room. 'I felt physically nauseated witnessing the pain of labour suffered by my wife Lorna,' he told the *Irish News*, but in the event the three children arrived safely. The future star of *Fifty Shades of Grey* lay in a nappy in a cradle, surrounded by admirers, and whilst the nappy and cradle would disappear, he was destined to continue to be surrounded by admirers throughout a great deal of his life.

Jamie was born into a very distinguished family, and his father Jim was well known in Northern Ireland as one of the best and most prominent doctors in his field, becoming the Director of Fetal Medicine at the Royal Maternity Hospital and subsequently Northern Ireland Tiny Life president. Professor Dornan, to give him his correct title, became a senior vice-president of the Royal College of Obstetricians and Gynaecologists and held chairs at both Queen's University Belfast and the University of Ulster, as well as becoming an international campaigner on women's health issues.

Jamie's grandparents on both sides of the family were Methodist lay preachers and his father Jim was the only son of Grandfather Jim, a great soccer player by all accounts, who was an accountant from Belfast. Grandfather Jim was the general manager of what was then known as the Cripples Institute in Bangor, and is now called the Northern Ireland Homes for the Disabled, an upbringing that profoundly affected the younger Jim's view of life.

Unusually at the time, Jim was delivered by a female doctor called Joy Darling. Perhaps it was an early sign that he would devote his life to working with women, delivering untold numbers of babies – in the thousands, at least – and addressing himself to the problems of childbirth. Jim's was by no means an ordinary childhood, though: he grew up in the Cripples Institute, which incorporated a children's home, men's home, holiday home and workshops, and he attended Bangor Grammar School. He was a lively child, and seeing so much hardship and suffering at close hand must have given him a sense of empathy that he never lost. He turned down a place at Trinity College, Dublin, and instead went to Queen's University Belfast, where he found gynaecology and reproductive systems 'the most exciting module I did by far' – had he not been a doctor, he would have become a teacher, he later admitted. At the time, there were still high mortality rates for small babies, and initially there were fears he would spend a lot of his life consoling bereaved mothers. As the medical profession developed over time, however, that didn't come to pass.

For whatever reason, Jim has always displayed an enormous empathy with women and, never short of female companionship, had girlfriends from an early age. However, it was when he met Jamie's mother Lorna, who was a nurse, that the time came to settle down, and they began to build their family, first the two girls and finally Jamie. It was a happy time. The young Jamie developed a passion for reading, which has never left him and, a sporty little boy, he started playing rugby at the age of eight and golf a few years later when he was eleven. He also developed a love of animals, and when he was young he set his heart on becoming a ranger. In fact, fate held a very different future in store.

Growing up in Northern Ireland, Jamie couldn't escape the everyday tensions associated with the Troubles. The political and sometimes violent ricocheting between Catholics and Protestants were still an issue when he was young and he, like everyone at the time, was affected by them. 'I think people from Northern Ireland have some kind of unspoken general feeling of what it is to be around segregation,' he told the *Daily Telegraph*. 'You have an awareness of it because you know how much grief it's caused. It's a tiny percentage who have ruined it for that country, and that pisses everyone else off? Jamie was a Protestant and the IRA was running a high-profile bombing campaign both in Northern Ireland and mainstream Britain. By the time he left home, the Troubles were largely coming to an end, but no one who has lived through that era ever forgets them. It would be ludicrous to link his childhood experiences with those of the troubled Christian Grey, but both men suffered trauma in their upbringing, and for Jamie, there was more to come.

While he was still a young boy, however, there was plenty of fun to be had. Theatrics ran in the family: both sets of grandparents included a lay preacher, and while they would probably not appreciate being compared to actors, such a role demands a certain presence and ability to present oneself as a creature on a stage. Jamie's father Jim was also a keen amateur actor and had briefly considered joining the profession himself when he was young. More impressive still, Greer Garson, a huge star in her day and best known for the 1942 production *Mrs Miniver*, was Jamie's great aunt. Jamie never actually met her, though he did write her a fan letter when he was a teenager, a letter she never had the chance to read as two days after he wrote it her death was announced on the radio.

Clearly, acting was in his blood, though it didn't become apparent quite yet. Passionately interested in sport and still dreaming of becoming a ranger, Jamie boarded at Methodist College in Belfast, known locally as Methody, a voluntary grammar school located in south Belfast. An academic institution, with a reputation for music and sports, especially rugby, hockey and rowing, it had a high Oxford and Cambridge entrance rate and boasted prominent alumni such as *Red Dwarf*'s Chris Barrie, television presenter Caron Keating and rugby players Craig Gilroy and Paddy Jackson, as well as several politicians, Nobel Prize winners, eminent poets, authors and diplomats.

It was also very much the sort of school that educated children who went on to pursue mainstream professions – not to become models turned actors. Jamie was well liked, however, and the school had a strong tradition of amateur dramatics, which is where Jamie continued to show early ability and promise, as well as a hint of what was to come. 'He was very modest,' Vice Principle Norma Gallagher told the *Radio Times*. 'One of his best subjects was drama. I remember him making a very good milkman in *Blood Brothers* and Baby Face in *Bugsy Malone*.' Jamie took his amateur theatricals seriously and began to appear on various circuits in Ireland, including playing a role in Chekhov's *The Cherry Orchard*.

Despite the tensions of the Troubles hanging over them, Jamie had a happy and privileged life in Belfast. Unlike some of his peers, he didn't have a gritty working-class background: his was one of privilege, from a comfortable and well-to-do home in the leafy suburbs of the city, complete with all the creature comforts anyone could want. In spite of this there was still no clear idea where he would go as an adult. The amateur theatricals continued, but that is all they were – amateur.

Jamie had been sporty since he was a young child and that

continued at Methody, where he played a lot of sport, something that helped build up the famous physique that would stand him in such good stead later in life. He particularly enjoyed rugby as a fleet-footed winger who could run the 100m in 11.1 seconds. His love of sport has remained with him as an adult, though he has admitted to never going to the gym. And when he was younger at least, he was able to get away with eating a lot of rubbish as all that running about allowed him to burn it all off.

It was at Methody that Jamie discovered girls, too. He had his first kiss at twelve or thirteen, he confided to *Fabulous* magazine: 'It was that classic of behind the bike sheds at school, when I was twelve or thirteen years old, with a girl whose name I can't remember,' he admitted. It was hardly a serious relationship, but it was a sign that women found him very attractive indeed.

For a happy boy with a sunny disposition, Jamie endured a great deal of tragedy at a tender age, which has left a tinge of sadness that's still evident at times today. The first dreadful event happened when he was just sixteen and his mother was diagnosed with pancreatic cancer. She died soon afterwards, sending the family into total shock. Years later, when he was asked how he coped, Jamie's father Jim stated bluntly that he didn't to begin with. The family was shattered. 'You can't prepare for that,' he said in an interview with the Irish television presenter Eamonn Mallie. 'It was completely and utterly and totally devastating to us all. But we managed to deal with it.' The loss of his mother at such a young age is something that continues to surface in interviews. It was one of the harshest things that could have happened to a boy who, though in his teens, was still really a child.

That wasn't the end of his misfortune, though, as within fourteen months four of Jamie's friends were tragically killed in a car crash – it was a further blow that would take years to recover from and which still comes up in interviews today. At the time it must have seemed as though there would be no end to the sequence of traumatizing events. 'I had a terrible time when I was sixteen, seventeen,' he said in an interview with the *London Evening Standard*. 'Therapy got me through that, actually; I'm not sure how I would have coped without it. It's awful to say this but it's almost better that I went through that early on because it's prepared me for situations that might arise later in life. Actually I don't know that it did, it's just some shit that happened.'

Jamie had lost his mother and his friends: his world view had changed and his life was shaken up. Therapy may have helped him to make some sense of what had happened, but the awful, incontrovertible facts remained the same. No matter how painful it was, though, life had to go on. Jamie was still at school, and he had to complete his studies and then, in time, decide what he was going to do in the future. The whole family had to learn to cope, and as their new reality sunk in, things returned to a version of normal.

There was yet more upheaval on the horizon, although this time it turned out to be positive. Jamie's father Jim met Samina Mahsud, another doctor, who went on to become his second wife in 2002. A consultant sub-specialist in maternal fetal medicine based in the Regional Unit at the Royal Maternity Hospital in Belfast, Samina was both twenty years younger than Jim and from a different ethnic background; differences that could have caused problems but didn't. At the time, in 1998, she had been working as a registrar for a friend of the Dornans; they had known Lorna as well, and thought that Jim and Samina would get along.

'He sort of knew that I would be quite partial to meeting her,' Jim later told Eamonn Mallie. 'He sent her up to listen to me – I was speaking at the Four Provinces meeting in Dublin – and she came up to speak to me and it was pretty instant for me, I must say. She is beautiful but she's very witty, very humorous, and it was her sense of humour that made me fall in love with her.' The attraction was immediate, with Jim recounting how he drove eight hours to Limerick to see her, but they didn't properly become a couple until the following year.

Once engaged, Jim had to meet her parents, always potentially nerve wracking and in this case even more so due to the age and cultural differences. Samina's family originated in Waziristan, a mountainous region stretching from northwest Pakistan to eastern Afghanistan. Jim had spent some time in that part of the world, in addition to which Samina's father had studied at Southampton University and was familiar with the ways of the West. Jim and Samina concocted a story to the effect that Jim was going to fly out to Pakistan in order to buy some furniture and, as he was a friend of Samina's, her father would collect him from the airport. In the event, Jim's future father-in-law guessed why Jim was coming and candidly advised him to look for a younger woman. Younger even than Samina. He was an illustrious figure himself, who had been in charge of power and water in Pakistan for twenty years, and he knew and respected an educated man when he met one. The families got on like a house on fire, perhaps aided by the fact that Samina's father had been brought up by Irish nuns. Sadly, in time both Jim's and Samina's fathers developed leukaemia, and whilst Jim's survived, Samina's father did not.

The couple were happy and everyone appeared to get on, but it must have been a difficult time for Jamie. He had lost his mother, and while Samina could in no sense be thought of as a replacement, it must still have been a difficult situation, and one that Jim was very mindful of. 'You know, everything about Jamie has made me proud,' his father told *Irish Central* after Jamie had started to make his name. 'The way he responded to his mother's death, the way he responded when four of his friends were killed in a car crash, the way he responded to the challenge of getting into the world he is in, the way he responded to my new partner and wife. He is an incredibly level-headed, solid guy. He's very well-rounded. I'm not just saying this, but he is one of the nicest people I know.'

Samina had a hugely positive influence on her new stepson, but in the meantime there was the minor matter of what Jamie was going to do next. With a background like his, university seemed the obvious step – although he had started dabbling in modelling, it hadn't occurred to Jamie to pursue it as a career, so after gaining A levels in Classics, English literature and History of Art, he enrolled at Teesside University to study marketing. Meanwhile, before his studies began, he had a couple of part-time jobs, working in a call centre selling gas and electricity – 'Hideous. I lasted a week,' he told *The Times* – and driving second-hand cars for an auction house. 'A low point. I only did a day of that.' Uni couldn't come soon enough.

Teesside University was situated in Middlesbrough in the northeast of England and was a newcomer on the academic stage, having gained its university status in 1992. Originally a technical college, it was a friendly enough place, with self-catering accommodation provided for first-year students like Jamie. This was the first time Jamie had lived in mainland UK, and he was able to sample at first hand not only student life, but life in England.

Right from the start, however, it was obvious that Jamie might be cut out for something more. For one, he was a winger for the Belfast Harlequins, and if he had any ideas at all about what he was going to do with the rest of his life, it concerned rugby, not modelling or acting. He was far more caught up in playing rugby than he ever was with studying, and after a fairly short time at university, he was pretty sure he'd made a mistake, having attended, he said, only nine hours of lectures: 'Nine hours too many. I didn't have a clue what they were talking about.' And so, having barely sampled the joys of academic life, he dropped out, intending to devote himself to sport. 'All I did was drink and play rugby,' he told *ShortList Mode*. 'I never went to lectures. I would not have set the marketing world alight had I qualified.'

But there was something else. Jamie was turning into a strikingly handsome young man – his father Jim had always been considered quite the dashing doctor – and everyone was beginning to notice it, not least his family. So when his sister Liesa spotted a commercial for a new show to be called *Model Behaviour* on Channel 4, she suggested her little brother try out for it. Jamie was intrigued and went along with a friend, then after the initial competition he was selected to go forward to the next stage. 'I got to the stage where there were five people from each different city that went down to London, I was one of the five people from Belfast, which isn't saying a lot,' he told *ShortList Mode*. 'I got to London – the idea was we were to be whittled down to the point where we were all living in a house together. I got kicked out on day two.'

Jamie played it down in later years but he acknowledged what a difference the show had made to his life. 'I wasn't too keen, to be honest,' he told *The Sunday Times*. 'It wasn't something I wanted to do. Back then I was playing a lot of rugby. I was a bit of a lad. Male modelling didn't really seem like the next step. So I persuaded a friend to go with me, and he came with me and didn't get asked back the next day. I was on my own from there, but it worked out quite well.'

Although he didn't make the finals, it was a significant

time for him because a number of modelling agencies spotted him and suggested he get in touch with the celebrity photographer Bruce Weber. 'He was good to me and gave me a couple of jobs early on,' he told the *Daily Mail*. Jamie also appeared on television and began to see for the first time what life in the spotlight was like, although in the early months it was pretty low key.

He may not have known it, but the early stage of his career was now underway, and in many ways it was a funny choice for him to make. Although he has toughened up after years in the spotlight, Jamie was originally a somewhat shy boy, totally impervious to any effect he might have on women. 'It's not like I cleaned up with girls,' he told the *Daily Mail*. 'I always looked young and I was very small – I hated being "cute".' His smallness, of course, would work to his advantage, as it does for women, since the cameras pile on the pounds; and while he was a little shorter than most models, like Kate Moss, with whom he would one day work and to whom he has often been compared, he wasn't actually that short by conventional standards. He was just a little slight. And as for being 'cute' – that was the reason Jamie first grew his beard.

Jamie might not yet have been considering a career in acting, but he was thinking quite seriously about trying to make it in music. In 2002 he got together with his best friend David Alexander, who he had known from school days, and the two of them put together an outfit called Sons of Jim (both Jamie's and David's fathers are called Jim). Jamie later dismissed their efforts out of hand, and it's true that they never got near the big time – although they did end up as a supporting act to K T Tunstall – but there was a certain appeal to their brand of folksy pop. The two of them certainly presented themselves as a couple of likeable lads: avowedly blokeish, they named the record label on which they would record a few songs Doorstop Records, after a sandwich shop in Belfast.

Eventually, Jamie came to the conclusion that he wasn't a good musician, and said that the two of them were young, naive and underprepared, but it was a sign, perhaps, that show business was where his future lay – or that he had an urge to perform at least. They did a little touring, appeared on television and made a small name for themselves, although ultimately the band never really took off. On the plus side, it gave Jamie more experience of television and more exposure to the spotlight. It was a case of living and learning what he wanted to do as he went along. And despite Jamie down-playing this episode in later years, the duo had quite a long shelf life, continuing after Jamie moved to London, where they cropped up quite a bit in between times as Jamie's modelling career took off.

What Jamie had wanted and assumed he would do was to become a professional sportsman, but as John Lennon once famously put it, life is what happens when you're making other plans. Neither sport nor music had taken off in quite the way he'd expected or hoped, but that initial appearance on *Model Behaviour* had alerted a few people to his potential. His initial contact with Bruce Weber had shown everyone that Jamie could be in demand, and it was actually

Samina – by now Jamie's stepmother – who realized that Jamie might be able to carve out a career in modelling. In order to do that, though, he would have to leave Belfast. To a certain extent that had already happened, of course, given that he had gone to the northeast to university, but that was in some ways temporary, and he always went home in the holidays. This was the real thing: a big break away from all that he had known. Jamie was a grown man by now, so he was hardly an innocent abroad in the big city. That said, however, he had spent his entire life in Northern Ireland, apart from his short stint at uni, and this was something completely new again.

In London, Jamie's life continued to fail to go to plan. He had a rotten time of it at first, before matters started to improve, as reflected upon in a newspaper interview he gave after he finally started to hit the big time.

'When I was younger I thought maybe one day I'd be involved in sport in terms of a career. I was also involved in youth theatre,' he told *The Scotsman*. 'Then, as you get a bit older and have to make decisions about roughly where you want to be and what you want to be doing, it just kind of happened. My dad was a keen actor when he was young, my auntie is heavily involved in amateur dramatics back in Northern Ireland and my great aunt was a woman called Greer Garson. She still holds the record for the longest ever Oscar acceptance speech, which is cool. So there's an element of it in the family. My dad was offered a place at RADA when he left school, and didn't take it. He became a doctor and had a very fulfilled life doing that, but I think there was always a part of him that wanted to explore acting, so I think he's probably as excited as I am that I'm doing it, because he gets to vicariously live that side of him.'

Finally, after the trauma of his teen years, Jamie was about to find success and happiness and, further down the line, love, too.

3

The Golden Torso

And so, like so many millions before him, Jamie decided to seek fame and fortune by moving to London. With his music career still bubbling away in the background, Jamie's thoughts about becoming a professional sportsman were fading. He still wanted to act, but nothing much was happening there either. One thing that was becoming clear to him now, though, was that he wanted to try his hand at modelling, although initially things didn't go according to plan.

Life in the capital can be tough and Jamie certainly found it so. He found a council flat in Hackney, east London, which may be a fashionable place to live but it can also be a very rough one. He had absolutely no money and for a short time life was very difficult, working in a pub to support himself and only just about managing to survive – at one point he shared a bathroom with twelve other people. There were few creature comforts, and it was a very different set-up from his childhood days. 'For some reason, despite the fact that it's so cheap, I felt like I couldn't afford a kettle – to make tea I'd just leave the hot tap running for ages until I got it scalding,' he told J. P. Watson in an interview on *jpwatson.com*. He couldn't even afford a decent television, making do with a wobbling black and white one. It wasn't exactly life in the fast lane. He visited Milan in the hope of picking up some work for the catwalk shows and had no luck. What modelling work he did manage to come by was mainly wearing naff-looking sweaters for catalogues. La dolce vita it was not.

This went on for six miserable months until Jamie's father Jim came to visit. Accustomed to his lovely home in the suburbs of Belfast, Jim wasn't thrilled to see the circumstances his son was living in, and matters got even worse when he asked to watch a rugby match. 'The picture kept flickering,' he continued. 'I sat with my dad, with a cup of tea I'd made from a rusty hot tap, watching this pathetic excuse for a telly. He just looked at me and said, "Son, you can't live like this," put his foot down and helped me get out of that situation.'

It was the kickstart Jamie needed. He began going for more jobs, after which slowly – and then quickly – work for the big names started to come in. In 2002 he was spotted by Select modelling agency, and soon he was appearing in magazines such as *GQ* and *Attitude*.

Most famously, he went up on Calvin Klein billboards where he posed with Eva Mendes, a campaign that earned him the nickname 'the Golden Torso'. Jamie was a little bemused. 'What does that mean? Is it a colour reference? I think it is meant to be a compliment. I hope it is,' he told the *Daily Telegraph*. Shoots consisted of 'a lot of people rubbing me down with dark, oily tanning stuff – I mean, I'm a white

Irish guy; it was a problem.' The Calvin Klein ads caused quite a sensation – in 2006 he was paired with Kate Moss for the campaign, which caused uproar because Moss was topless. Not for the last time, Jamie was spoken of as the male equivalent of Kate, and it's true that both of them have a slight quirkiness that makes them stand out from the crowd.

The really famous names were starting to flood in: Dior, Armani and a campaign for Asprey where, on a shoot in Manhattan in 2003, he met Keira Knightley, the former child star who had become a well-known actress in the film *Bend it Like Beckham*. The two were soon a couple, although they kept it quiet for a while, and Keira introduced Jamie to her agent, something which would prove helpful when he finally started to make a breakthrough with his acting career. The start of their relationship was not without trauma, though: Keira's ex, actor Del Synnott, was said to have taken an overdose (later denied) when they split up. There were rumours that Keira wanted a break in her new relationship with Jamie to recover from the shock, but it wasn't long before they were back on track. It was Jamie's first taste of the limelight, as Keira was, after all, a massive star, and *The People* contacted him in New York to find out what was going on. 'To be honest I am not really allowed to talk about it,' he said. 'Basically my agency have said if anyone calls me I have to forward all calls onto them. I can't [talk about it]. I'm sorry, I really can't.'

The names on Jamie's modelling CV continued to pile up – Hugo Boss, Nicole Farhi and Massimo Dutti, as well as Gap. Jamie wasn't exactly famous, as most models, especially men, are not household names except in exceptional circumstances, but his face was certainly familiar. Magazines, billboards – you name it, Jamie was on it more often than not, gazing out from magazine pages and looking thoughtful. In fact, he was developing something of a trademark serious look.

So what did everyone back in Belfast make of it all? 'It wasn't exactly what my dad expected of me,' he told J. P. Watson. 'A lot of his mates thought it was embarrassing that I was having my picture taken for money. I'd grown up playing a lot of rugby and they all probably thought it was a wee bit nancy boyish.'

Jamie was getting pretty good at it, though, pouting this way and that and fast becoming the best paid male model in the world. It irked him that he was so widely thought of as an underwear model, given the number of other jobs he did fully clothed. He still wanted to make the break into acting, but this new and slightly unexpected turn of events was proving to be a very lucrative sideline, and so Jamie took the pragmatic approach: while behind the scenes he was trying to break into acting, he took the work that was offered while it was there. Did it offer fulfilment? No. But it kept a roof over his head.

'I've never felt massively satisfied from standing there while someone takes my photograph,' he told the *London Evening Standard* some years later when he'd finally got into acting. 'It's never given me a thrill [but] it would take a very foolish man to turn down the stuff that was offered to me.

You're in your twenties, and people are going to give you a silly amount of money to lean against a wall with your head down. F*** me, you've got to do it.' And do it he did. His days of not being able to afford a kettle were a distant memory now.

It could have gone to his head, but it didn't. His close family ties helped keep his feet on the ground and his naturally modest and self-deprecating nature was the ideal foil to a world in which appearance is everything and where people often start to believe their own publicity. Jamie wasn't like that at all. Not only did he not go along with some people's opinion that he was the best-looking man in the world, he didn't think he was particularly good looking at all. 'I don't like my physique,' he told *Interview* magazine. 'Who does? I was a skinny guy growing up and I still feel like that same skinny kid.' But that's not what everyone else saw. Now massively in demand as a model, Jamie was on the verge of making the next major breakthrough: recognition beyond the industry. When the public started to know who he was, he really was on his way.

That was still some way off, though, and his words betray an insecurity, something that would have an effect on his personal life. In 2003, it became public that Jamie and Keira were an item, which increased the interest in him even more. Keira, who was born on 26 March 1985 and was thus a couple of years his junior, was brought up in show-business circles – her father was the actor Will Knightley and her mother the actress-turned-screenwriter Sharman Macdonald. Keira began acting as a child, made her film debut in 1995, appeared as Sabé in *Star Wars Episode I: The Phantom Menace* in 1999 and, while she was with Jamie, found huge, global international stardom courtesy of the massively successful *Pirates of the Caribbean*, in which she played Elizabeth Swann opposite Johnny Depp's Captain Jack Sparrow. So their romance coincided with Keira's ascent to the A list and all that that entailed.

For the first time Jamie began to see what life was like in the limelight – at least at one remove – and he wasn't totally thrilled by it. Keira was a huge star and paparazzi followed her everywhere. Everything she did, said and wore was a matter of interest for the public, and it took Jamie aback to see the attention she was subjected to. 'Being with Keira was an insight into how rotten the whole thing can be,' he told the *Daily Telegraph* some years later. 'A young girl is being followed around the street, there is nothing positive to say about that.'

On another occasion he spoke about it to the *Standard*. 'It was a strange environment to find yourself in, being hounded and followed,' he said. 'It's really hideous. Fucking hell, [the paparazzi] are cretins. I couldn't have less respect for those guys. There are so many ways to make a living that don't involve hiding in bushes opposite houses of eighteen-year-old girls with a camera in your hand. That's not making a living, that's making a choice to be a perverted fuckhead. That scrutiny when you're older will be easier to take. And I don't think I'm ever going to be as famous as her.'

Now that Jamie has signed up for one of the most

high-profile film roles in years, it has caused friends to worry about how he will manage with the level of attention that brings. Jamie is absolutely every bit as likely as Keira to become paparazzi fodder and there are some people who are concerned how he will cope.

At this time, though, it was simply a matter of dealing with Keira's growing popularity. In 2004, she was voted the sexiest movie actress of all time in a poll by *Empire* magazine. Of the two of them, Keira was very much the catch. She seemed to be working very hard to keep the relationship quiet: although they were often pictured together, at a premier for *King Arthur* Keira was on the red carpet alone, while Jamie accompanied her mother. They even kept their distance at the post-premiere party, until Keira got a little tipsy.

'Keira and Jamie spent most of the night apart and it wasn't until Keira admitted she was finding it difficult keeping upright due to the champagne that they retired to a sofa and he nuzzled his face in her hair,' a fellow guest told the *Daily Express*. 'It was really only once she was a bit tiddly and had done all her required schmoozing that she allowed herself any time with him. She kept laughing about being tipsy but she was really very controlled considering it was a huge premiere in her honour. And rather than let herself go, shortly after sitting on the sofa, she, Jamie and her mum left via a back door.' He also had to put up with all the rumours and speculation that are part and parcel of having a relation-ship with a famous star. There were constant (false) reports that the couple had split up, that Keira was close to her latest co-star, Adrien Brody, that all was not well and that they had then reconciled.

Only the very strongest relationship can withstand that sort of pressure and with the best will in the world Jamie and Keira were still extremely young, barely starting out in life and working in an intensely pressurized industry. Far stronger relationships had collapsed under the weight of such pressure in the past. As for Brody, the main reason for the rumours about him and Kiera appeared to be that the two of them had had the occasional drink when they were out filming *The Jacket* in Glasgow – which was enough to provoke headlines such as 'Keira's got ex appeal'. It can't have been easy to live with. Then again, it was good practice for the moment when Jamie himself would bear the full brunt of the limelight.

As matters progressed Jamie and Keira turned up to openings and premieres, sometimes dressed up to the nines and looking young and gorgeous, and at other times covered in mud and getting very much in the spirit of things at Glastonbury. It was Jamie's first big relationship, and for a while it was very serious: the two adored each other and saw one another as much as they could, which could be difficult given that both of them had busy schedules modelling, acting and generally making a pretty good show of being one of the best-looking couples in the world. They even met each other's parents. Would they go the distance? Could Jamie and Keira actually be thinking about settling down?

In 2004, when Jamie was twenty-two and Keira nineteen,

he moved into her flat in Mayfair, central London. Keira, who at the time was starring as a somewhat battle-hardened Guinevere in the film *King Arthur*, was happy to tell the *Sunday Mirror* about their relationship: 'Jamie's great, I'm mad about him,' she said. 'He keeps me sane when things get stressful and we always have fun together.' What about marriage? 'I'm way too young,' Keira said hastily. 'One day in the future maybe, but marriage and kids are just not on my mind at the moment.' Nevertheless, the two of them were frequently pictured all over each other; they clearly fancied one another something rotten. Was it really about to go wrong?

Not quite yet. Friends of Keira's talked about how much she 'idolized' her boyfriend, and the two were seen shopping for furniture for their new home. Then Keira provoked speculation by commenting, 'I don't know if I'm in love,' before commenting on the charms of George Clooney. This was followed by calling her co-star in *King Arthur*, Clive Owen, 'a lovely kisser! Great! We did quite a few takes and he's very good,' in an interview with the *Daily Record*. She was clearly only doing it in an attempt to deflect the intense speculation surrounding her and Jamie, but it only had the effect of increasing curiosity about their relationship. Of Jamie, she said, 'He's great, very sweet and sexy. We have a lot of fun together, but I don't want to talk about him really. Let's just say we're really happy together.' Whether or not she wanted to talk about the relationship was not the point, though – everyone else did.

Perhaps inevitably, wedding speculation began. The *Daily*

Mirror carried a report that they had been seen looking at engagement rings: 'They were spotted strolling around Bond Street the other day looking in shop windows at diamond engagement rings,' said a source. 'Keira seemed to have her eye on something pretty special and she's told her friends she'd love to get married sooner rather than later. They also visited a jeweller in Harrods, but the store was sworn to secrecy and promised not to talk. It seems they are preparing to get engaged, or maybe they've already done it and kept it a secret.' The same report also referred to rocky spells in the relationship, though, so it was impossible to know what was going to happen next.

Sometimes matters surrounding the two of them descended into farce. When they attended a party for the *King Arthur* film in the City of London's Guildhall, Keira had been loaned £250,000 worth of jewellery by Asprey to wear for the occasion. But the crush at the party was such that the security people couldn't stay close enough to ensure that no one tried to steal the jewels. As a result, they got to her at midnight and took the gems, prompting the inevitable comparisons with Cinderella. 'I was really quite frightened; security rushed in here at midnight and took my necklace and bracelet,' she told the *Daily Express*. 'I felt like Cinderella turning into a pumpkin at the last stroke of the clock. But it was a relief to give them up – it was terrifying having all these people crushing around me when I was wearing all that money. I was really worried that someone was just going to snatch it from around my neck.' Jamie, of course, was present and saw the madness at first hand.

Such was the fuss surrounding her that it was easy to forget that, far from being an experienced Hollywood diva, Keira was still only nineteen. Fame had come so suddenly that she had been forced to learn how to deal with it, especially the huge surge of public attention, while at the same time cultivating a fledgling relationship. It would not have been an easy balancing act for anyone, let alone someone so young. 'I haven't stopped working, so I haven't had time to take a step back and assess things,' she told the *Daily Telegraph*. 'Obviously there are differences now: getting on the bus is becoming a little difficult, but I'll work through that. It's also strange when people recognize you in the street and they know you but you don't know them. It's a little weird, but nothing to complain about.' It's safe to say that Keira wouldn't be taking many more buses in the future. She was, however, managing to remain pretty down to earth about it all, though there was no question that her life had changed beyond compare.

Inevitably that didn't just affect her; it also affected Jamie. He was doing perfectly well in his career – stunningly well, in fact – but two such impossibly glamorous people in a relationship couldn't help but attract attention. As Victoria and David Beckham have so beautifully illustrated, a couple can be far more than the sum of its parts, and while one A-lister will always be of interest, two A-listers in a relationship is far,

far better. Jamie might not have been an A-lister then, but Keira certainly was, and it was clear that he was also heading that way fast.

Increasingly they were spoken of as the next golden couple, a fact that only added to the pressure. 'To make it in the eyes of the celebrity magazines you need to have the boyfriend and the love interest,' said Kirsty Mouatt, editor of *New!* magazine. 'I imagine her boyfriend will start getting a lot more breaks from being associated with her and they will become the next super couple.' And there it was: the suggestion that Jamie would benefit professionally from his association with Keira. It must have rankled.

Comments like this highlighted the fact that there was another issue to deal with. Jamie and Keira did not at that time enjoy the same status. Jamie may have been a mightily successful model, but his was not a famous name, whilst Keira was famous all over the world. That meant that although Jamie was one of the world's best-paid male models, he couldn't equal Keira in terms of earning power, a fact that began to take its toll. Worse still, the papers often reported on the fact that Keira had introduced him to her agent and was hoping to find a film role for him, something that would have made Jamie feel even worse. It was bad enough that he wasn't an equally big star, but for it to be implied that if he ever did make it, it would be because of Keira was hard to stomach. Even the most well-adjusted men can find it hard to play second fiddle to a woman and Jamie was having to do so on several counts, as he was neither as famous nor as well paid as his girlfriend. For the time being, however, he coped.

As Keira's fame grew, she could at times be very coy, telling one reporter who asked about the status of the relationship, 'Nobody I'm going to mention. I'm not going to mention anyone until I'm married to them. I'm far too young to think about a serious relationship – I imagine it would be quite difficult with this job.' It was a bit disingenuous considering she had already mentioned Jamie in the press, and on the very same day she was quoted elsewhere as saying she was mad about him. No one likes the thought that they're being swept under the carpet, and none of this would have helped matters in the long term. All Jamie could do, though, was get on with life and endure it, but the more his girlfriend got caught up in the publicity maelstrom, the more difficult he found it.

Stories continued to swirl about the two of them. It was said that when Keira was filming *King Arthur*, she had fallen in love with Ireland and was looking for a house in Dublin, which would have been handy for Jamie's family in the north. It was also reported that she had been spotted visiting the Dornans over Christmas 2004 in Belfast. Early in the new year she flew to the Caribbean to start work on the *Pirates of the Caribbean* series. Jamie visited her there and they were seen nuzzling one another in various exotic locations, so the relationship still appeared to be going strong.

At times, though, the pressure of living in the public eye seemed to be taking its toll. In an interview with *The Sunday*

Times, Keira point-blank refused to talk about Jamie: 'I am completely happy talking about my family, as in my mum and dad. But it would be foolish for me to start talking about relationships at this age,' she said. 'So until I have a husband and couple of kids I'm going to keep schtum about any marriage plans.' As usual, the interview was with her and not her boyfriend. Was Jamie similarly keen to keep quiet about his famous paramour? No one knew because no one was asking. Tensions behind the scenes were beginning to build.

One friend gave an insight into the pressures the two were facing. 'Keira is a very private person and she's decided not to do any interviews about her relationship with Jamie,' he told the *Mirror*. 'They have been in the newspapers so much recently and have decided that drastic action is needed. The best way of stopping the speculation about them marrying is for Keira to stop answering questions about Jamie in her interviews.'

In mid-2005, Jamie was, for once, the focus of attention when it emerged that he had filmed a role in the forthcoming film *Marie Antoinette*, of which more anon, and that Sons of Jim had signed a contract with Sony. 'It's a sizeable role,' said a spokesman for Jamie's agent to the *Daily Express*. 'It's certainly not blink and you miss it. It's just finished filming in Versailles and he thoroughly enjoyed making it. Jamie is an actor but he's also a musician. His primary focus is his music.' It was then put to the spokesman that Jamie was largely known for being Keira's boyfriend. 'Well, I would dispute that.'

Jamie of course was delighted that at long last he'd be getting a share of the limelight, but was all really well behind the scenes? 'By this time next year I could be as hot as Keira is now,' he was reported as having said behind closed doors. 'It's better to be in an equal partnership.' That was perhaps the biggest warning note that something was wrong. Their unequal status appeared to be becoming a very big issue for Jamie, and matters weren't helped by rumours that Jamie had enjoyed flirting with his co-star Kirsten Dunst. It must have been as unsettling for Keira as it had been for Jamie when rumours about Keira and her co-stars had circulated. She was used to being the star in the relationship and it must have been difficult watching her boyfriend, no matter how much she wanted him to succeed, claiming her ground. Something was bound to give – and it did.

4
Celluloid Tales

I n the end, the inevitable happened and in August 2005 the pair split up. It was an immensely traumatic time for them both: they had been together for two years, and despite their youth it had been a serious relationship. In the end, though, the pressures became too much. Not only were they under constant scrutiny, but they were both in professions that compelled them to fly all over the world at a moment's notice and now, to cap it all, there seemed to be an element of competition between them. It was all too much.

'Keira's gutted. She really thought what she and Jamie had was love but it just wasn't meant to be,' a friend told the *Mirror*. 'They both wanted it to work but in the end it was just untenable. They were having crisis talks on an almost daily basis but the decision was reached to finally call it a day. When Jamie announced that he wanted to broaden his repertoire and try acting as well as modeling, Keira was totally supportive. Keira arranged an interview with her own agents and she was genuinely delighted when he was signed up. While the idea of them both sharing the same profession was romantic, the reality is that they were starting to see less and less of each other. Keira's one of Hollywood's most in-demand actresses and her schedule is really punishing. When she comes back from a shoot she shuns showbiz parties and enjoys a quiet life with people she loves around her. But with Jamie trying to crack the big time he's not often around – especially as he's also been trying to land a recording deal. That's very hard for a young couple to withstand.' Keira appeared to be coping, though. 'She's already been on the town with the girls for a couple of boozy nights out, and although she's still distraught it has done her the world of good.'

A spokesman for Jamie confirmed they had separated: 'Keira and Jamie have decided to call a halt to their relationship in its current phase but they remain completely committed to each other as friends and will continue to see each other in this capacity.'

Jamie was pretty honest about it at the time, although he would later regret the manner in which he went public about their problems. It turned out that one of the fundamental problems in their relationship was that Jamie felt he had a lower status. Many men would have felt the same, and he simply couldn't keep pretending everything was all right.

'There is a big pressure when you go out with someone like Keira,' he told the *Mail on Sunday* several months later, after the dust had begun to settle. 'You can feel a bit second-rate and that's what started to happen. It's not like I was bringing the bread to the table – and that can start to affect everything. The man is meant to be the Alpha in the relationship on the money and power front and clearly I was not. You feel you have to be dominant in other areas and that leads to problems. Keira could see what I was going through and it would have been better if I'd kept it hidden from her. It's a slow process, trying to be this Alpha Male.

'The person who finally said, "OK, that's it, I've had enough," was Keira. But I think it was the culmination of many factors. To be honest, I'm not sure I noticed Keira's huge rise – I'm not sure she did either. She's the most beautifully grounded person I've ever met. I'm coping fine but I do feel very hurt at times. Things could be worse, couldn't they?' In later years, though, when his own career had taken off and he was becoming a 'name', he regretted those words, concerned, perhaps, that he came across as a little resentful or unkind to Keira. But at the time, that was the way he felt, and it had to come out.

Keira herself was a little more muted, as indeed she had been throughout their entire relationship. 'We all need romance in our lives but marriage and living happily ever after is not something I think about at the moment and certainly won't for a while,' she told the *Mirror*. 'But who knows. It's a nice dream.' She was not, however, immune from talking about what she would look for in a man: 'I'd go for someone who is a little bit brooding and somebody you can have a good conversation with, a good fight with, who will always keep you guessing and make you laugh. And he has to have good shoes.' In the event the two of them were spotted together shortly afterwards, but the body language revealed only that it really was all over. It was rumoured that they'd been having rows on a daily basis, and things certainly seemed to have run their course.

Keira spoke again at a little more length, to *Now!* magazine, explaining what had finally led them to split. 'Things change slowly and it isn't simply a matter of moving on,' she said. 'A relationship, as every girl knows, is complicated. It's not black and white – it's various shades of grey. So there's no way to explain what happened in a paragraph. There's no way you can explain a relationship. To anyone reading this I'd say, "Try it." You're looking at a whole set of complex issues. All I can say is that I'm extremely happy because I've been able to stay friends with every person I've had a relationship with. It's something that you read and don't believe, but in my case it's true. I'm lucky in that I have a great group of mates and I can do my talking to them.'

It was time, as they say, for everyone to move on, although in actual fact the former couple didn't, at least not straight away. They might have decided to part but they were still clearly determined to maintain some sort of friendship, and so they were still often seen together, with Keira attending a Sons of Jim gig and Jamie helping her pack. For now, at least, they were managing to maintain their friendship and, to this day, neither has said a bad word about the other.

It had been Jamie's first really serious relationship and the break-up, in 2005, took its toll. He was asked if dealing with his mother's death had given him the strength to deal with it, but unsurprisingly, perhaps, the answer was no.

'Losing Keira is a different kind of grief,' he said. 'The strength I got from losing my mum isn't helping me deal with it. When you feel that you've lost someone it's very hard.'

He was extremely honest about how cut up he was about the split, and this was also evident in a song he wrote at the time, 'Only On The Outside', which contains the lyrics, 'I can see your fancy friends trying to steal your innocence ... You're so weak around them.' Even several years later the song seemed to have an effect on him: 'The song hurts so much when I sing it,' he told *OK!* Australia. 'We were so in love.'

In the aftermath of the split the attention, just as it had done when they were together as a couple, centred on Keira. She had a new film coming out, *Pride and Prejudice*, in which she played Lizzie Bennet and Jamie attended the London premiere. Beneath all the hurt and upset, though, there was a new sense of freedom. Jamie was now quite sure he wanted an acting career and, slowly at first but with increasing momentum, that was what he set about doing. He was also still singing, and Sons of Jim were about to release a new song, 'Fairytale'. It told of an 'angel eyes' who 'leaves me when it's just right'. 'Maybe happiness is just another fairytale,' it went on. No prizes for guessing who might have inspired those lines.

'To tell you the truth, Keira was always just somebody's girlfriend to the rest of us, not this big star,' said Jamie's Sons of Jim bandmate David Alexander to the *Daily Star*. 'She is still in close contact with Jamie and the two of them are still very good friends. Probably because we're a duo, we've been compared with Simon and Garfunkel, which is a great compliment.' It was possibly a slightly misplaced compliment, but Sons of Jim were battling to make it in the music industry and were spending a lot of time in the studio, which, if nothing else, kept Jamie's mind off his recent woes.

As well as his music, his modelling career was going from strength to strength. The Golden Torso was everywhere, in 2006 signing up with Creative Artists Agency in Los Angeles, and flying all over the world for yet more shoots. His modesty remained, though. 'I question why all of this has happened to me,' he told the *New York Times*. 'I don't see myself as particularly good looking.' Everyone else did, though. 'In the span of twenty years, I've seen maybe four models who have what Jamie Dornan has,' said Jim Moore, creative director of *GQ*, in the same article. 'He's like the male Kate Moss. His proportions are a little off. He has a slight build. He's on the small side for male models. But his torso is long, and so he looks taller, and he brings a relaxed quality to modelling. He knows what he's there for, but unlike a lot of people he's not trying to be a male model. He is not modelling.'

David Farber, the style director at *Men's Vogue*, agreed. Jamie had posed with Kate for the Calvin Klein jeans campaign, with both of them appearing topless, and Farber pointed out that this 'was effective casting. It got people's attention. Clearly he wasn't the typical model.' He was 'real', he explained. 'But obviously he wasn't some skinny waify model boy they found on the street.'

Jamie continued to profess bewilderment at it all. 'Why am I the face of Dior Homme?' he enquired. 'At Dior, they kept eliminating people until it was down to two. I wasn't really focused on it at the time, you know. I don't really know why Hedi [Slimane, the Dior designer] chose me. I'm not the best-looking guy around. The reason it's all worked out so well for me is that I don't take it all too seriously.' In that he was almost certainly right. Unlike some of the female super-models, Jamie wasn't in the slightest bit difficult to work with and was always utterly professional. There were no airs and graces at all.

Meanwhile there was growing wealth in the background. Jamie had by this time managed to buy a house and a flat in London, no mean feat for someone still in his early twenties. Nor was it just his torso that was admired: people were talking of the 'Dornan furrow' – the pout he put on when he was modelling – and, good sport that he was, he would put it on for interviewers if they asked nicely.

His relationship with Keira was over, but their years together had not only given Jamie a lasting distrust of the paparazzi; it had also given him an insider view into the life of a successful actress and film star. This was the life Jamie had wanted for himself for years, and being so close and yet so far can only have added to his sense of frustration at not being able to get what he wanted. Added to that was the prejudice that many casting agents have against models who want to become actors, which is a problem in the UK, though not so much in the States. There, it's accepted that people do what they have to do to earn a living and be recognized, and it isn't assumed that all models are brain-dead idiots who can't do anything else. They are just as likely to be talented in other fields as anyone else – only in their case, they are lucky enough to look good, too.

As his modelling career progressed, Jamie had been going to tens if not hundreds of auditions behind the scenes, but with relative lack of success. Given the difference in attitude towards models who want to be actors on either side of the Atlantic, it's perhaps no surprise that Jamie's first opportunity came in the United States when, in 2006, he got his first film role in the aforementioned *Marie Antoinette*, directed by Sofia Coppola. 'I'd been auditioning for parts for years,' Jamie told *Interview* magazine. 'I never got any better at it. I'm crap at auditions. I know there are people who can walk into those rooms and make the lines sing on the page and get the job immediately. I wasn't one of them. I'm still not one of them. Even after I got my first acting job, thanks to Sofia, I still went a while without working. If you ever wonder why some actors end up taking shit jobs, it's because they have to pay the mortgage – or because they just want to work.'

Still, it was a start. Sofia, who had made her name with the film *Lost in Translation*, was directing a film called *Marie Antoinette*, based on the life of the doomed French queen although, to put it mildly, the plot took massive liberties with historical reality. Maria Antonia Josephina Johanna Habsburg, portrayed by Kirsten Dunst, is the beautiful and naive princess of Austria, and the youngest daughter of Empress Maria Theresa's (Marianne Faithfull) sixteen children. In 1768, she is selected by her mother to marry the Dauphin, the future Louis XVI of France (Jason Schwartzman), in order to seal an alliance between their two countries. Marie Antoinette duly goes to France, where she meets King Louis XV of France (Rip Torn) and her future husband, Louis Auguste. The two arrive at the palace of Versailles, which was built by the King's grandfather, and are married and encouraged to produce an heir to the throne as soon as possible. Alas, there is no success.

Marie Antoinette is not happy at Versailles, not least because she is a foreigner who hasn't managed to produce a child. She has to deal with gossip and somewhat tactlessly refuses to meet with the Comtesse du Barry (Asia Argento), who is the mistress of Louis XV. On top of this, Marie's attempts to have sex with her husband fail and the marriage remains fruitless. She spends most of her time buying shoes, dresses, jewellery, luxurious pastries and gambling. Then the King catches smallpox and orders du Barry to leave Versailles. He later dies and Marie Antoinette becomes queen.

Her brother, Joseph II, the Holy Roman Emperor (Danny Huston) comes to visit, counselling her against her constant parties and associations; advice that she ignores. Joseph then meets Louis XVI and explains to him the 'mechanics' of sexual intercourse in terms of 'key-making' (one of the King's favourite hobbies is locksmithing). That night, the King and Marie Antoinette have sex for the first time, and on 18 December 1778, Marie Antoinette gives birth to a daughter, Princess Marie Thérèse of France. As the baby princess grows up, Marie Antoinette spends much of her time at the Petit Trianon, a small chateau in the grounds of Versailles.

She also begins an affair with a dashing Swede named Axel von Fersen (a beardless and at that point totally unknown Jamie). As France's financial crisis worsens, food shortages and riots become commonplace. Marie Antoinette's image with her subjects has completely deteriorated by this point, and her luxurious lifestyle and seeming indifference to the struggles of the masses earn her the title Madame Déficit.

Chastened, she modifies her behaviour, and a few months after her mother's death on 29 November 1780, Marie Antoinette gives birth to a son, Louis Joseph, Dauphin of France, on 22 October 1781. Another child, Louis XVII, follows on 27 March 1785, and another daughter, Princess Marie Sophie of France, on 9 July 1786, who unfortunately dies on 19 June 1787, a month shy of her first birthday. As the French Revolution rapidly begins to erupt, the royal family unwisely resolves to stay in France. Angry rioting Parisians force the family to leave Versailles for Paris. The film ends with the royal family's transfer to Tuileries Palace and a shot of Marie Antoinette's bedroom, destroyed by angry rioters.

The film, which was based on a biography of the real Marie by Antonia Fraser, a considerably more sympathetic portrayal than the usual 'let them eat cake' image, was filmed in and around Versailles and had a mixed reception, although it has since become something of a cult classic.

'Everything we did is based on research about the period, but it's all seen in a contemporary way,' Sofia told *Cinema-review.com*. 'My biggest fear was making a "Masterpiece Theatre" kind of movie. I didn't want to make a dry, historical period movie with the distant, cold tableau of shots. It was very important to me to tell the story in my own way. In the same way as I wanted *Lost in Translation* to feel like you had just spent a couple of hours in Tokyo, I wanted this film to let the audience feel what it might be like to be in Versailles during that time and to really get lost in that world.'

The film created a lavish world, dripping with, in Sofia's words, 'beautiful flowers, enormous cakes, silk and tassels,' and Antonia Fraser herself loved it. 'I adore the look of the film,' she told *Cinemareview.com*. 'I thought it was magically beautiful. It's something film can do that I could never do. I can write page after page about the beauty of Versailles and the grace of Marie Antoinette, but on film it's so much stronger.'

Some reviewers were not entirely sure what to make of it all. Leah Rozen, in *People* magazine, said of its Cannes Film Festival reception, 'The absence of political context, however, upset most critics of *Marie Antoinette*, director Sofia Coppola's featherweight follow-up to *Lost in Translation*. Her historical biopic plays like a pop video, with Kirsten Dunst as the doomed 18th-century French queen acting like a teenage flibbertigibbet intent on being the leader of the cool kids' club.'

The *Chicago Sun Times*' Roger Ebert was kinder, giving the film four out of four stars. He wrote, 'every criticism I have read of this film would alter its fragile magic and reduce its romantic and tragic poignancy to the level of an instructional film. This is Sofia Coppola's third film centring on the loneliness of being female and surrounded by a world that knows how to use you but not how to value and understand you.'

In France, the critics also had mixed feelings. Danielle Attali of *Le Journal du Dimanche*, praised it as 'a true wonder, with stunning colours, sensations, emotions, intelligence.' François Vey of *Le Parisien* found it to be 'funny, upbeat, impertinent . . . in a word, iconoclastic.' And that was very much the view that prevailed over time. Philippe Paumier of the French edition of *Rolling Stone* said, 'Transformed into a sanctuary for the senses, the microcosm of power becomes this moving drama of first emotions and Marie Antoinette, the most delicate of looks on adolescence.'

But Jean-Luc Douin of *Le Monde* was not so keen, calling the film 'kitsch and roc(k)oco', saying it 'deliberately displays its anachronisms', and was a 'sensory film' that was 'dreamt by a Miss California' and 'orchestrated around the Du Barry or Madame de Polignac playground gossip'. Perhaps, though, it was unsurprising that some French critics would take umbrage at an American view of French history. Alex Masson of *Score* thought the film had a script 'which is often forgotten to the corruption of becoming a special issue of *Vogue* devoted to scenes of Versailles'.

French historians didn't like the way Sofia had played fast

and loose with history either. In *Le Figaro*, historian Jean Tulard called the film 'Versailles in Hollywood sauce': it 'dazzles' with a 'deployment of wigs, fans and pastries, a symphony of colors' which 'all [mask] some gross errors and voluntary anachronisms.' In the magazine *L'Internaute*, Évelyne Lever, whose special subject was the late queen, sniffed, 'In reality she did not spend her time eating pastries and drinking champagne . . . In the movie Marie Antoinette is the same from fifteen to thirty-three years . . . better historical films, including *Barry Lyndon* and *The Madness of King George*, succeeded because their directors were steeped in the culture of the time they evoked.' In other words, don't mess with a culture you don't understand.

The film has subsequently garnered a far more positive reputation than it did at the time of its release (it was plain that Sofia was not actually trying to convey the exact historical reality, but merely using it as an inspiration) and Jamie's role, in truth, was not a great deal more than a cameo, but it was a start. There was bemusement in some quarters that the Golden Torso should have landed such a role, but why not? Jamie himself had learned of it from his agent while rehearsing with Sons of Jim, flew to Paris and found out the next day that he'd got the part. 'It was the last role cast,' he told the *New York Times*. 'I guess there had been pressure to have a certain ilk of actor, some big name from the up-and-coming list, but they hadn't been able to find someone.' They had, however, found Jamie, who at long last achieved his goal: to appear in a film.

'It was amazing to work with such talented people on my first film,' he told the *Sun*. 'Kirsten Dunst is a fantastic actress – perfect to play French queen Marie Antoinette. Our sex scenes were a lot of fun. My chest was naked but I kept my pantaloons on below! Kirsten had to perform in bed wearing slippers while holding a fan, which was bizarre. But the director, Sofia Coppola, had everything under control and I think she's made a great job of the film.' Jamie even met Sofia's father Francis Ford Coppola. 'I was watching the filming on the monitors and next to me was one of the best directors in the world. I had to pinch myself.'

While it would be pushing it to say the floodgates for acting roles opened in the wake of the release of the film, Jamie had been on screen for long enough to prove a point: he could act. He was to complain in later years that his looks held him back, but for now he had shown that not only did he look good on screen, he had talent, too. Interestingly, Jamie's appearance as a model was very much linked to the bearded look, but his debut on the silver screen was free of facial hair – it seemed that producers and directors did not agree with Jamie's view of himself, namely that he looked better when his face was framed with a beard.

There was real hope for a future in acting now, even if it did take a little while for his career to properly take off. Jamie still had his modelling, which he could rely on to earn money, but his name was at last being linked to further acting projects. He was making a good impression, too. Jamie didn't take himself too seriously and had a self-deprecating streak that meant a fair few people fell for his charm (another quality he'd inherited from his father). After years of lurking on the sidelines and seeing the highs and lows of fame through another person's eyes, it was Jamie's turn. He had proved he had what it takes, and now he was on his way to becoming a major star.

5

Succès de Scandale

The break with Keira was made and Jamie's film career was launched. Suddenly Jamie found himself in a very different place to the one in which he'd been less than a year ago, and his role in *Marie Antoinette*, while small, was the launch pad to a career that would shortly take off in spectacular fashion. His career as a model was by no means over, though, and in 2006 he was attracting as much attention for modelling as for anything else he did.

In the spring of 2006 it was announced that Jamie would once again be modelling for Calvin Klein, having done so previously in 2004, but what marked out this particular campaign was that he would be appearing alongside Kate Moss. It wasn't just the alignment of two beautiful people that made the news, however: what made this worthy of comment was that the year before Kate had been pictured allegedly taking drugs, acquiring the nickname Cocaine Kate in the process and prompting dire predictions that it would herald the end of her modelling career. In fact, the opposite had happened, and after a short stint in rehab and the loss of a few contracts, Kate bounced back with a vengeance.

The Calvin Klein contract was particularly important for her because it was their 1992 campaign that had turned Kate into a household name, when she'd appeared in a series of black and white shots alongside Mark Wahlberg. She worked with the designer until 1999 and now she was back with a deal said to be worth £500,000 and a dinner held in her honour. 'Kate and the Calvin Klein brand have a long history together and it felt natural to reunite them for this new Jeans campaign, which will inevitably reignite that spark and highlight the sexy, cool essence of both Kate and Calvin Klein,' said campaign creative director Fabien Baron. The campaign was to be shot in New York. 'I had never met her before but she is really a lovely person – very nice and more shy than you'd expect,' Jamie told the *Mirror*. 'But when you are working with someone who is at the top of their profession it is a real thrill.'

As usual, all the attention was focused on the woman at his side rather than on Jamie himself, but why should he care? His career was on the up and he was enjoying himself; he was even spotted having a drink with none other than Lindsay Lohan at Hollywood's Koi club. That in itself was a healthy move, as in the months after their break-up, Jamie and Keira had been photographed together so often there were constant rumours of a reconciliation, with the result that neither of them had really been able to move on. Now, finally, Jamie was being seen out with other women. Even if this particular outing didn't turn into anything serious, it was a start. In fact, the two were reported to be dating, although that may have been overstating things – some years later, when a list of Lindsay's alleged conquests came to light, Jamie's name was on the list.

Jamie was quick to deny there was anything in it. 'I'm not dating Lindsay Lohan. I did read it though and I thought it was funny,' he told the *Mirror*. 'I know who she is. I've seen *Mean Girls* but that's it. I am as single as they come. There's no Mrs Jamie at all. I have just never been very good at meeting girls in general because I am quite shy when it comes to women. I have never been one for chatting someone up. And I think it's quite hard to meet someone special in London – there is a whole pool of attractive women in London but I find it quite intimidating. London is so vast so it makes it hard to know where the nice ones are or what kind of people they are going to be. It was a lot easier when I was at school and you knew everyone you pulled. I've been single for about six months, which is quite a long time, too long maybe. But that doesn't mean I haven't had fun and there are always girls I'm attracted to.' Indeed. The capital's womenfolk could only hope. On the domestic front, he was now sharing a place with his sister Jessica in a new flat in Notting Hill.

Alongside his modelling, Jamie continued to play with Sons of Jim. 'We've been good friends since school and it wasn't a conscious decision to form a band together. Sons of Jim just developed organically,' his friend David told the same newspaper. 'I remember Jamie and I used to get up and sing covers of songs we loved at parties – everything from the Beach Boys to Bob Dylan. And we are fortunate enough to have a group of mates who appreciate good music – they encouraged us so we eventually began writing our own songs.' The duo were to release a new single called 'My Burning Sun' on 29 May and hoped to release an album in October.

'"My Burning Sun" was written to uplift us a bit because we were both very fed up with winter and wanted summer to come,' Jamie explained. 'We write everything together and as far as who takes the lead vocals it's fifty fifty, so I'm definitely David's other half as far as Sons of Jim goes. I always sang, and from the age of about sixteen I used to write stuff. I didn't know if it was poetry, lyrics, whatever. I just used to write it and then gradually I started to sing bits of it. I was aware I had some kind of voice and I did drama with some singing involved, but I wouldn't have classed myself as a singer until Dave and I started doing stuff together . . . I'd love everything to succeed – I want Sons of Jim to be a success, still have a successful modelling career and succeed at acting as well. I don't see why I can't do all three – if you try really hard to make all these things work I don't see why it can't work out. If I am doing a film I might have to take time out from being in the recording studio as I might be away on set. But when it comes to modelling, it isn't like you're away on month-long assignments – it doesn't take that long to take a photo. You are only away for two or three days here and there and a lot of the time you are in London anyway. I find it quite easy to balance things – and I still have a lot of spare time to do nothing as well, which is nice.'

In the end some of his wish would come true, although in truth the music career never really got off the ground.

By this time Keira had been linked to her *Pride and Prejudice* co-star Rupert Friend, and as a single man-about-town, Jamie was discovering that he need only talk to a woman for them to be linked to him in the press. The next name to feature beside his was Lucia Giannecchini of *Footballers' Wives*. Kate Moss had also been spoken of as a potential girlfriend, entirely on the grounds, it would seem, that they looked so good together, but Jamie was dismissive, pointing out that the same rumour mill had attached him to Natalia Vodianova when he worked with her the previous year. 'I'm not cool enough for Kate,' he told the *Mirror*. 'I've met her several times and she's really sweet but I somehow don't think I'm rock star enough. Given her taste in men I'm just not her type.' His sex scenes with Kirsten had been pretty raunchy, too, so of course her name was added to the list, as was Sienna Miller's, for no other reason than that she was young and gorgeous. Lily Aldridge was a name that also featured, although friends denied that anything serious had happened between them.

Jamie took it all in his stride. 'I know the girls who I've been linked with, but that's all there is to it,' he told the *Sun*. 'If you're seen out together, people automatically think you're a couple. Of course that's not the case. I'd be a very lucky guy if all the stories were true!' But if he was interested in someone . . . 'I make the best spaghetti bolognese in the world,' he said. 'If I was trying to impress a girl I'd probably whip up some spag bol and serve it with a nice bottle of red wine. But, as I said, there's no one special at the moment.' He was telling everyone that he was over Keira, but it was hard not to suspect there was a flame still burning there.

Meanwhile he had also started to deny that 'Only On The Outside' was written with Keira in mind: possibly it had occurred to him that the lyrics were a little unkind. 'Considering Dave and I write together, I can't work out how that could be true,' he protested to *The Sunday Times*, and elsewhere he claimed to have only said the song was difficult to sing because it was hard to reach the high notes.

The single shadow cast over an otherwise enviously happy existence was that back in Belfast, his father Jim had been diagnosed with leukaemia. Given how young Jamie had been when he'd lost his mother, his anxiety was palpable. 'He's been ill with leukaemia for a while and despite all the treatment he still isn't in remission,' Jamie told the *Sun*. 'Dad's an amazing guy. My mum Lorna died from cancer of the pancreas when I was only sixteen. She had been ill for about a year and a half. Afterwards Dad helped me pull through the grief. He is the strongest person I have ever met. It's lovely that I can respect him through the name of the band.' In time, Jim would make a full recovery, but it was a worrying period for the whole family.

Meanwhile Jamie's romantic aspirations continued to be a source of fascination. Models Gemma Ward and Lily Donaldson were said to be in the frame as girlfriends, as were various Geldof sisters – had Jamie really been dating this lot there would have been no time for anything else. Mischa Barton was another contender, mainly on the basis that they'd been seen chatting at a nightclub. He was also seen talking to Lily Allen at the V Festival in Chelmsford, where they swapped numbers. But again, it proved to be a false alarm. To top it all, Jamie was named a gay icon and featured on the cover of the US gay magazine *Out*.

There was only one name that Jamie was repeatedly linked to, though, and it was beginning to annoy him. They had, after all, split up. 'People knew me in the fashion world before I started going out with Keira because I've done some good work but it's proving hard to lose the stigma that's attached,' he told the *Sunday Mirror*. 'I can't shake off the title of Keira Knightley's ex-boyfriend. It frustrates me so much because Dave Alexander' – his bandmate in group Sons of Jim – 'and I have been writing music together for five years, before I even met Keira, and getting places with it and creating awareness.'

In the meantime, rumours continued to circulate about Keira's love life. There was constant speculation that she had split up with Rupert Friend and further conjecture that Jamie was secretly pining for her. When Jamie was linked with Sharleen Spiteri, it was yet another rumour that turned out to be totally false. He also shot an Aquascutum campaign with the Brazilian model Gisele Bündchen, although in this case it was so patently obvious there was nothing between them that, for once, they weren't linked. Nevertheless, they made an arresting-looking couple: Aquascutum chief executive Kim Winser said, 'The campaign portrays a week-end of stolen moments, intrigue and trysts. Gisele and Jamie are the perfect pairing to communicate our creative vision for the new season.'

Jamie maintained his equilibrium. 'Me a supermodel? Nah. I mean, people aren't really interested in male models that much are they?' he was heard to observe. Supermodel or not, the women he was shooting campaigns with certainly fell into that category and he was more in demand than ever, spoken of as part of a new wave of male models (together with David Gandy) who exuded personality together with good looks. Now that he was no longer with Keira, the pressure was off slightly, in that he wasn't so constantly followed by the paparazzi, even if he did still get accused of dating every woman he spoke to. Alexa Chung was the next to be named after the two were spotted chatting at the V Festival, but as usual, the rumours were groundless.

The Keira connection continued into the autumn of 2007, when she had another film out, *Atonement*, and although she was at that stage well and truly ensconced with Rupert Friend, Jamie's name continued to be mentioned in the roll call of her life. It was frustrating for Jamie, as his acting breakthrough proved illusive following *Marie Antoinette*, and he continued to forge ahead with his modelling career.

He was still well known enough to be deemed worthy of inclusion in prime-time television, though, although not yet in the acting roles he would later pursue so well. Along with the likes of Gary Rhodes, Jenny Bristow, Rachel Allen and former Miss Universe Rosanna Davison, Jamie was recruited to take part in *The Fabulous Food Adventure*, in which various celebrities travelled around the food-producing regions of Northern Ireland before taking their spoils back to be cooked by Anthony Worrall Thompson in a signature dish for each county. It might not have been a Hollywood blockbuster, but it was profile-raising all the same.

At around this time came the announcement of another breakthrough – Jamie was to star in *Beyond the Rave*, a Hammer horror starring Sadie Frost as a vampire. Inevitably, when the news came out Jamie was described as Keira Knightley's ex, but there was the feeling that he was starting to emerge as a name in his own right.

His modelling continued, and Jamie was name-checked in a diary by the model Daisy Lowe during London Fashion Week: the two were on the same table at the Elle Style Awards, and Daisy called Jamie 'really hot'. He was also considered well-known enough to be included in a round-up by the *Observer* on the tricks of buying vintage clothing: 'When I see something I like in a vintage shop, I hide it,' he said. 'I saw this great Beach Boys T-shirt for twelve pounds in Beyond Retro in London and hid it with the jackets. I went back just in time to see some guy pick it up, hold it up to himself and bloody buy it . . . I bought a brown suit in Belfast's Rusty Nail just to spite my friends really, who said it was nasty. I grew to love it . . . Vintage clothes feel nicer when they're worn in a bit. They're just . . . softer . . . There are downsides to wearing vintage clothes, of course. I've had a couple of shirts with bad armpit situations.' All of which seems sound advice.

In the end it was just as well he hadn't given up the day job modelling, as when *Beyond the Rave* was finished in early 2008, it turned out Hammer had produce a turkey. Reading the plot it wasn't hard to see why. Jamie – who played the lead role, Ed, a soldier due to fly to Iraq – sets off in search of his girlfriend Jen, who was played by Nora-Jane Noone. Imagine his dismay when he finds that she's been sucked into a crowd of undead party goers, all intent on making her one of their own. The rave was, natch, in the middle of a deep dark wood, and thrown into this nonsense was Ingrid Pitt, a star of some of the legendary Hammer films of yesteryear, and the afore-mentioned Sadie (as a 'fallen angel'). Given that this was Hammer's first film production since a remake of *The Lady Vanishes* in 1979 – before Jamie was even born! – it wasn't anyone's finest hour.

Initially Jamie was very enthused. Was this, at last, going to turn him into a household name? 'I had just come out of a nice family period drama, and that was partly why I wanted to do something like *Beyond the Rave*. I was also intrigued by the whole webisode thing,' he told the *Daily Telegraph*. 'The shoot felt a lot faster than anything I'd done before. There was a real buzz on set because everything was so speedy. But then, if you're going to make an impression in a five-minute epi-sode, it's got to be pretty sharp. It was new territory for everyone.' And what about the blood? 'Well, it was quite hard to take it seriously when you're being attacked by a mad vampire wielding two samurai swords.' Perhaps that was the trouble. If the actors involved couldn't take it seriously, it was unlikely anyone else would.

In later years, when he had a body of work he could genuinely be proud of, Jamie was asked how on earth he got involved in the film. 'I met the producer at my sister's wedding and was very fond of him,' he told *Interview* magazine. 'I liked what he was trying to do with the project, and after plenty of drink, I said I'd be involved. Then I was involved and it was a mad shoot. The whole thing was a night shoot. I was sleeping all day, having no life, and then getting up, going to work at six in the evening and coming home at six in the morning – very strange. I don't remember a great deal about that time, [laughs] but I made good friends. We were brought together through the lack of sleep.'

The director was Matthias Hoene. 'I grew up watching Hammer,' he told the *Daily Telegraph*. 'It was always exciting to see that mix of horror and sexiness . . . On the one hand there are the old fans who will always think that something new won't be as good. But we really wanted to do something fresh that would capture a young audience, so we set out to tell a story that's thrilling and sexy and a bit shocking.' And deeply, deeply silly.

Another innovation was that the whole thing went straight to the internet, to MySpace, where it was broadcast in five twenty-minute 'webisodes'. This carried its own unique demands. 'Normally in a feature film, you would spend the first ten or fifteen minutes setting up the characters and the background,' Hoene continued. 'But in this project we had to ensure that every five minutes there would be character development, thrills, fun – the whole package that you'd expect from a full-length film. And, of course, not every episode could end in a cliffhanger – that would be too forced . . . If you want to watch something short during your break or while you're on the bus, if you want to be entertained for just a little while, it's perfect. This is just another way of telling stories. Dickens wrote serialized stories – were they bad for being short? It can be a great format. What I love about horror is that you can take certain serious subjects – political, social – and talk about them in an entertaining way that would be impossible in another sort of drama. You can deliver messages in a horror film that you couldn't otherwise. If you made a straight film about genetic experiments, for instance, no one would go to see it. If you made a horror film with the same theme, a lot of people might. Do it intelligently and you'll get your message across.'

Alas, despite all the high-mindedness, it didn't turn out to be the ground-breaker everyone was hoping for. Clips leaked out on to the internet and viewers were not kind. 'I managed to get a look at this and it was cheap, cheap, cheap – a low-rent throwaway cash-in on the Hammer name,' wrote one. 'Really terrible,' wrote another. 'An awful load of shite.' Director Matthias Hoene valiantly defended his creation: 'It's a young and fresh product which uses young actors and a young crew and brings up young talent,' he protested to the *Sunday Mirror*. No one was convinced. Jamie gamely tried to reassure readers of the same paper that it wouldn't be too gory: 'There's only one way you can chop off a head,' he confessed. 'But I don't think this is as over-the-top as Hammer. There are gory bits kind of related to how it was when Hammer used to do it.'

It was no good, though; nothing was going to save this misconceived production. Given that the budget was estimated at about £500,000 – a sum that wouldn't cover the catering budget for a Hollywood extravaganza – perhaps no one should have been surprised at the way it turned out.

There was also a so-bad-it's-good school of thought, as demonstrated in Jaci Stephen's review in the *Guardian*. 'The head of the vampires is Melech (Sebastian Knapp), who takes a shine to Jen and wants her to go in the vampire-mobile (or whatever transport vampires use) to an island, where they will all live happily ever after,' she wrote. 'We leave tomorrow for distant shores,' he tells her. 'Is there a berth with your name on it?' Knapp is hilarious – delivering ridiculous lines with the air of seriousness that such nonsense requires – but the real laughs belong to the Crocker brothers, a threesome of complete ineptitude who try to take on the vampires in several bouts of gang warfare. "We're in a bit of bother 'ere, aren't we?" they note after accidentally kicking a loose head in the middle of the road.' There was a great deal more in this vein, but the reader was left in no doubt that it was risible viewing.

No career is without its hiccups, though, and Jamie was swift to move on. 'I'd love to do a comedy with Angelina Jolie,' he told the *Sun*. 'It's harder to be a leading man in a rom com if you're not English. I think the English do that really well – that sort of slightly camp, slightly pathetic thing.'

At least he was on the Hollywood radar now, and he was fast becoming known for more than just modelling. Projects were, slowly but surely, building up in the pipeline and Jamie was starting to make contacts, seeing scripts, meeting directors and moving into the world he wanted to inhabit. He was also going to lots of auditions, and more often than not failing to win the part, but he was determined, hard-working and able, and it was starting to feel like it was only a matter of time.

There was still no new girlfriend on the horizon, though, and friends of Jamie's were beginning to wonder why. After all, he was a very attractive bloke, who had been linked to some of the most beautiful models in the world, so why, several years after the split with Keira, was he still finding it hard to find a new girlfriend? Plenty of people were of the opinion that Jamie hadn't got over Kiera, an impression he may have been responsible for, but which only emphasized his loyalty to those he cared about. When asked by the *Sunday Express* why there was still no significant other, he replied, 'I'm a loyal person. I hate the idea of even switching banks. Even though I could be saving money, I really like the guy at my bank, so I just couldn't let him down.' If he felt that strongly about his bank manager, how much more would it apply to his ex, the first major relationship in his life? It might have irritated him that people still spoke of him in connection with Keira, but it looked a lot like she had made a lasting impact on him that had yet to fade.

In a strange way, it was another preparation for the role of Christian Grey. Christian was, after all, troubled, harbouring emotional wounds, and a damaged soul. It's been said that it was only after Frank Sinatra lost Ava Gardner that he was really able to sing torch songs. Was the split with Keira Knightley to become the trauma that turned Jamie into the actor he is today?

Jamie Dornan first found fame as a fashion and underwear model, working on campaigns for Calvin Klein, Dior and Armani, among others.

With his modelling career in full swing, Jamie began rubbing shoulders with A-listers.

Jamie's 'golden torso' on display.

Jamie has been linked to several glamorous actresses, including Mischa Barton (*top left*) and Sienna Miller (*top right*). He dated actress Keira Knightley from 2003 to 2005.

His real-life Anastasia: Jamie eventually found love with actress and singer-songwriter Amelia Warner.

The happy couple married in 2013 and have a baby daughter.

Jamie's breakthrough acting part was playing Count Axel Fersen in *Marie Antoinette* opposite Kirsten Dunst in the title role.

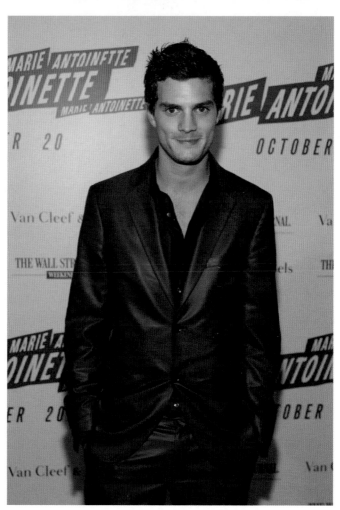

Jamie steps into the limelight at the premiere for *Marie Antoinette*.

Jamie modelling one of his signature smouldering looks during a New York fashion shoot.

From strength to strength: following his role in *Marie Antoinette*, Jamie began to feature in more high-profile projects. Seen here in ABC's *Once Upon a Time* playing the mysterious Sheriff Graham Humbert.

Jamie explores his dark side while playing serial killer Paul Spector in the drama series *The Fall*.

A rising star: Jamie receiving the Best Actor award at the 2014 Irish Film and Television awards for his critically acclaimed performance in *The Fall*.

6

Nice to Meet You

J amie was nearing the moment when his acting career would properly take off but he wasn't quite there yet. There was still more forgettable work to come and the next was a real oddity, a short film called *Nice to Meet You* starring the mother and daughter combo of Trudi Styler and Mickey Sumner opposite Jamie in the role of brooding, nameless hunk. The plot, such as it was, involved Jamie turning up in Trudi's garden (none of the characters had names) on the run from the police. She provides shelter for him until the police have gone, at which point there's a will-they-won't-they moment, interrupted by the arrival of Trudi's daughter. Jamie scarpers, but when said daughter brings home a new man shortly afterwards, who should it be but the refugee from the law? There's more smouldering between mother and potential son-in-law, which is brought to a swift and merciful conclusion by the end of the film, although it's never made clear whether the two succumb to their illicit desires.

As tosh it was right up there with *Beyond the Rave*, but for particularly keen fans it's now up on YouTube. Jamie was under no illusions about the film, though, telling one interviewer that he couldn't believe she'd seen it. Nor had that many seen *X Returns*, another curious short, filmed at around the same time and revolving around a mysterious Agent X (Jamie), who escapes his Los Angeles cell after forty years of false imprisonment and scientific testing and must backtrack over forty years to find out what happened to his family and previous life. The film had a cast of five as opposed to just the three, but at eleven minutes running time it was never going to set the world alight.

It was all good experience for what was to come, though, and what followed next was in a different league altogether. *Shadows in the Sun*, starring the legendary Jean Simmons – it was to be her last film – told the story of how a young loner heals a family having to deal with the pain of watching an ageing relative decline. Joe, played by Jamie, is a troubled soul who lives like a tramp in the 1960s and becomes involved with Hannah, an elderly widow who lives in a remote East Anglian location. Joe brings her cannabis to ease her pain, but problems arise when her son Robert, played by James Wilby, starts to mistrust his motives, with tensions rising further when Joe befriends Robert's daughter.

Jamie and James were both a little overawed to be working with Jean Simmons, who was something akin to Hollywood royalty, and this seemed to amuse Simmons. 'I'm not sure what they were expecting, some diva from Sunset Boulevard perhaps,' she told Allan Hunter in the *Daily Express*. 'I like to think I've always kept a sense of reality. I think that's down to my family and especially my brother, whose attitude about me was always, "Oh good, the kid is working." ' She was certainly down-to-earth and unaffected, much like her two young co-stars.

The film, which was written and directed by David Rock-savage, premiered at the Dinard British Film Festival, where it was met with some acclaim. 'Shadows in the Sun is a moving, beautifully realized and ultimately redemptive film about family, memory, forgiveness and love,' said Carey Fitzgerald, the boss of High Point Films, which acquired distribution rights for the picture – it was also a major step forward in Jamie's career.

Inevitably, however, the real focus of attention was Jean Simmons. Coincidentally, the film appeared in the same week as the re-release of Spartacus, originally made in 1960 and also starring Jean, leading Philip French to write in the Observer, 'The cinema confers immortality and it also traces ageing and helps us accept our mortality. The two come together in Shadows in the Sun, where the terminally ill old woman played by Simmons sees, just before her own demise, an al fresco production of The Tempest, a wise play commenting on departure and death.'

Andrew Pulver in the Guardian took a slightly less positive view. 'Director and co-writer David Rocksavage, aka the 7th Marquess of Cholmondeley, works hard to create a mood of understated wistfulness, so much so that his film ends up verging on the inconsequential,' he wrote. 'Nice performances all round keep things ticking along, but they're not helped by irritating devices such as the students performing *The Tempest* on a nearby beach.'

Tim Robey in the *Daily Telegraph* was also a little lukewarm. 'Tiny things happen oversignificantly in this indulgent British effort set in 1960s East Anglia, where a family converge to spend the summer with their lovely old gran (Jean Simmons),' he wrote. 'To complete this well-meant wallow in luvvie nostalgia, we get a picturesque shipwreck, much repetition of Schumann's *Traumerei*, and some passing players put on a valedictory performance of *The Tempest*.'

However, many more were completely won over by the film's gentle charm. Derek Malcolm in the *London Evening Standard* was one. 'This film is so far from the rough and tumble of most present offerings that one fears for it at the box office, but it is warmly shot by Milton Kam and, as family tensions mount, it creates an almost Chekhovian atmosphere, albeit in a very English kind of way,' he wrote. '*Shadows in the Sun* unfurls as quietly as a mouse and could be accused of lacking urgency and bite. But it is well played, particularly by Simmons, who still has the charisma of a star turn, and Wilby, and manages to hold the attention throughout. No one could deny that its heart is in the right place.'

Sam Jordison of Channel 4 Film wrote, 'It's all worked out with a quiet skill that won't have you hanging on the edge of your seat but will keep you intrigued and involved. It's thoughtful, it looks good and the actors do full justice to their well-rounded characters. Simmons steals the show with an understated performance that shows all Hannah's quiet resolve and warmth, but she's given excellent support by the rest of the cast.'

Allan Hunter's take on the film in the *Daily Express* was similarly complimentary: 'Simmons brings her charm and intelligence to the role of Hannah, an ailing matriarch who now lives alone in Pear Tree, the rambling country house she once shared with her late husband. Her companion is young handyman Joe (Jamie Dornan) who also supplies the cannabis that alleviates the pain of a long illness . . . *Shadows* is an understated tale that could have used a little more fire, but Simmons' presence helps to make it touching.'

Whilst the film didn't exactly set the world alight – 'Gran goes a little potty' was the *Sunday Mirror*'s headline – it was nevertheless a significant step forward for Jamie. Slowly and surely, the public's perception of him was beginning to change – he clearly had talent and this was soon to be showcased to a much larger audience.

Though Jamie was clearly on his way now, many reviewers still couldn't resist commenting on his looks. He was a model, after all, albeit one who exhibited some acting talent, and in Britain, as he so glumly noted on numerous occasions, there is still some suspicion attached to models who go into acting.

In January 2009, Jamie made it to number four on the list of Ireland's sexiest man, produced by *Social and Personal* magazine (television star Baz Ashmawy was number one) with reports of the 'hot young hunks' partying together at a celebratory bash. This was followed up by making it into the top ten of *Company* magazine's fifty most eligible bachelors in Britain – he was in good company as Prince Harry topped the poll. As ever, he continued to be linked to an ever-growing list of women: the latest was *Harry Potter* star Emma Watson, with whom he was seen chatting at the Grey Goose after-party at the Grosvenor House Hotel. Emma had been publicly worrying about the fact that she was about to have her first screen kiss with fellow star Rupert Grint, and was lamenting her lack of technique – as you can imagine, there was no shortage of suggestions that Jamie might be just the chap to help.

It was suggested that Jamie might be really interested in Emma, although it was notable that on the night in question she also spent time talking to three other men: Robert Pattinson, Nicholas Hoult and Alex Pettyfer. Would she succumb to any of them? 'Emma has blossomed from a cute and gawky teen into a ravishing movie star beauty,' an insider told the *Sunday Mirror*. 'She has no shortage of admirers and Jamie is one of them. She's a bit of a romantic, so he'll have to do it the old-fashioned way – lavish her with chocolates and flowers. He isn't used to girls saying "no" to him so he will keep trying. When he meets her at the next showbiz bash, he will try again. Last time, all the guys were making moves on Emma, so Jamie knows he has to be a bit quicker.' Then again, perhaps he was just enjoying her company. After all, he was young, free and single, and thoroughly enjoying his life.

His modelling career was still going strong, with Jamie appearing in Calvin Klein ads alongside Eva Mendes, who seemed to be having a fine old time writhing around all over him whilst topless, using Jamie to shield her modesty. Unsurprisingly, the campaign received a great deal of attention and Jamie's profile shot higher still.

He could, however, be a little oversensitive about how people judged him. Beautiful women are often perceived as having little intelligence and it turns out that exactly the same applies to very handsome men. As unfair as that might be, no one's going to hire Kate Moss for her brainpower, although she is by all accounts a very savvy businesswoman, and exactly the same applied to Jamie. It was something he couldn't help but complain about.

'People assume you're stupid enough as it is. Then you take your shirt off and they're like, "He must be an idiot," ' he told the *Sunday Mirror*. 'Seriously, people approach me and you can see it in their eyes. They speak to you very s–l–o–w–l–y. They're like, " 'Let's talk about grease and oil on your body. And aftershave. And your grooming technique." I understand: I mean, if I saw a picture of me, I'd probably be the same.'

Jamie revealed that a lot of people automatically assumed he was gay, too – clearly not the ones who read the endless speculation about his love life – and grumbled about the number of people who expected him to disrobe at the slightest opportunity. 'I'm not going to take my shirt off every time I'm in front of a camera,' he said. 'It's very accessible. Google "Jamie Dornan torso" and there you are. I've done it enough that I really don't see how it's interesting any more.' He did, however, relent: 'I've never bought that "my body is a temple" s**t, although mine does help pay my mortgage.'

Jamie adopted a considerably lighter note when being interviewed by the *Observer* in the wake of a shoot for *Men's Health*, which had just become Britain's biggest-selling men's monthly. That was in part because of men like Jamie, who were being judged on their looks in the same way women have always been. So what was his take on it all? 'I just think: men being idolized because they look good in pants – that's a bit ridiculous, isn't it?' he said, relating the tale of a man who had just asked him for an autograph and called him an inspiration. 'I found that weird. Signing my own crotch, thinking: Don't be inspired by a man who happens to look all right semi-clothed. There are so many other things you could be inspired by. I mean – it's OK to be inspired by a woman in pants! Ha! Oh dear . . . not that I'm suggesting that women's only purpose is to look good in pants . . .'

Unlike many female models, however, Jamie was a little more fortunate in what he could eat and drink. 'I've always needed to bulk up, so until the modelling took off I was ramming burgers down my throat and doing plenty of body-weight work – and drinking Guinness,' he told *Men's Health*. That wasn't really an option for his female counterparts.

By the autumn of 2009, Jamie had reached such a level of success in his modelling career that he was deemed capable of launching the careers of other male models, too. He launched the Calvin Klein casting event 'Nine Countries, Nine Men, One Winner', in which he was also a judge. The contest territories included England, France, Germany, Greece, Holland, Italy, Russia, Spain and Sweden. The judges had to select one finalist from each country, who would then compete against each other in a grand finale in March the following year. The prize was a modelling contract with Select Model Management plus a trip for two to South Africa, and in the event the winner was a fellow Brit, Laurence Cope. Laurence, nineteen, was a sportsman like Jamie, playing football and tennis, and became the latest to take on the international modelling stage.

In January 2010, it was announced that Jean Simmons had died. Jamie was badly upset by the news and paid her a very generous tribute. 'She was, what, seventy-nine when I worked with her?' he told *Interview* magazine. 'And when I think of all the films she was in, and how thoughtful and generous she was . . . I have to be careful here, because I was almost gonna tear up. She started as a kid. She had so many great stories. She worked with Marlon Brando and Frank Sinatra – in the same movie! I'm sure she got sick of me asking her about that. She told me one of her first jobs was as Vivien Leigh's stunt double. They rolled her up in a carpet and threw her into a pool for a scene where Vivien was to be drowned. She said she stayed underwater for what to her seemed like forever, but when she came up, she knew it was only a few seconds. She laughed about it, then she went from that to starring in *Spartacus*!'

Jamie was about to make a major breakthrough, but not before he had appeared in another blink-and-you'll-miss-it short entitled *The Black Widow*. By now, though still only in his late twenties, he'd come an incredibly long way. One of a handful of male models whose name was known to the public, Jamie was becoming quite wealthy, too. In 2011 he took part in modelling campaigns for *Wonderland* magazine, Gap, Desigual and Hugo Boss, and then the breakthrough he'd been so hungry for finally came his way.

Nothing in life ever goes entirely according to plan and so it should be no surprise that although Jamie had been lobbying hard to get into the film industry, it was actually two television series that eventually sent him on his way. *Once Upon a Time* is a marvellously innovative drama from Edward Kitsis and Adam Horowitz, two writers who had honed their skills on *Lost* and *Tron: Legacy*, and who therefore knew something about cliffhangers and how to keep people on the edge of their seats. The stories took place in two locations, fairyland in the past and real life in the present, and every character had a counterpart in the other location.

The show was set in the seaside town of Storybrooke, Maine, in which the residents are characters from various fairy tales and stories, who had been taken to the real world and robbed of their original memories by the Evil Queen Regina (Lana Parrilla) using a powerful curse obtained from Rumpelstiltskin (Robert Carlyle). Regina is mayor of Storybrooke, where the inhabitants have lived an unchanging existence for twenty-eight years, oblivious to the fact that they are not ageing. The town's only hope lies with a bail bondswoman and bounty hunter named Emma Swan (Jennifer Morrison), the daughter of Snow White (Ginnifer Goodwin) and Prince Charming (Josh Dallas), who was transported from the Enchanted Forest to the real world as a baby before she too could be cursed. As such, she is the only person who can break the curse and restore the characters' lost memories.

She is helped by her son, Henry (Jared S. Gilmore), with whom she has recently reunited after giving him up for adoption at birth, and his book of fairy tales, which holds the key to ending the curse. Henry is also the adopted son of Regina, providing a source of both conflict and common interest between the two women. Each episode usually has two segments: the first details a particular character's past life, adding another piece to the puzzle about the characters and their connection to the events that preceded the curse and its consequences. The other, set in the present day, follows a similar pattern with a different outcome, but also offering similar insights.

The new show premiered on 23 October 2011, with an episode in which the wedding of Snow White and Prince Charming is gatecrashed by the evil Queen Regina, who announces that she will put a curse on everyone so that only she will have a happy ending, at which point most of the fairy-tale characters are shipped to Storybrooke. At the end of the first season Emma Swan, the offspring of Snow White and Prince Charming, manages to break the spell. But when it came to season two, the producers had realized they had a hit on their hands and, wanting to continue the suspense, didn't allow the characters to return to fairyland, but instead forced them to deal with the knowledge of their dual nature instead.

It was into this intriguing scenario that Jamie stepped as the love interest of both the good guy (or rather girl) and the bad one. Things were definitely heading in the right direction for him at this point. Not only was this a major, prime-time US show, but he was acting with people of the highest calibre, including Robert Carlyle, in the dual role of Rumpelstiltskin/ Mr Gold, and with whom he quickly became friends. 'Bobby's a legend on every level,' he told *Fabulous* magazine. 'You know a great actor when it's all so effortless. We bonded quickly – a lot of people from Belfast and Glasgow do because they're similar places.' Another was Ginnifer Goodwin, who had found fame on the television series *Big Love*, about a fundamentalist Mormon family that practises polygamy, and who had been cast as Snow White.

The series was an immediate success. 'The idea for the show really started over eight years ago, when Eddie [Kitsis] and I had just come from working on *Felicity*,' said Adam Horowitz in an interview on *collider.com*. 'The seed of it was that we were trying to figure out what it is about storytelling that we really love, and what we love is the mystery and excitement of exploring lots of different worlds. Fairy tales clicked with us because they were so much in the DNA of what made us storytellers to begin with. If we can go between two different worlds and see two different sides of these characters, for us, as writers, that was a new way to explore characters and what makes them tick, and come at them from different angles. What you always want, as a writer, is to find different ways to explore the characters, and that's what got us excited about this idea.'

But writing about the dual nature of the characters in the fairy-tale past and the real-life present wasn't easy. 'That's the challenge,' he explained. 'Right now, we've got twelve episodes to try to do the best we can, to tell the coolest stories that we know how to tell, and it is an incredible challenge. In coming from *Lost*, we didn't want to try anything that was easy. So, we'll do our best and, if we succeed, great. If we fail, at least we're doing something that's challenging to us as writers.'

It was an absolute coup getting Robert Carlyle to sign up – indeed, the two men confessed elsewhere that they didn't initially think he would agree to star in the show – and his magnetic presence on screen unquestionably contributed to the show's success. 'What's amazing about our cast, and the casting for this, is that everyone we wanted, did it,' Horowitz continued. (With one exception. They revealed that they had offered the part of the Blue Fairy to Lady Gaga but never heard back from her.) 'That's no joke. We went to Ginnifer Goodwin. We went to Jennifer Morrison. We went to Robert Carlyle. We sent them the script and we said, "Would you want to do it?" and unbelievably they all said yes. It was very heartening. For us, with this pilot, there's been this sense of enthusiasm from everyone. Everyone who signed onto the show did so because they wanted to do it, and they're excited about the material. At least, that's what they've told us, so I'm choosing to believe that. And, because of that, there's this incredible energy of, "Let's all try to raise our game and do our best work." '

It was a tremendous challenge for the actors to play dual roles, as well as being one for the writers, and everyone involved was aware of that too. 'That's what's exciting, both for the actors and for us, as writers,' said Horowitz. 'We're able to constantly play with the duality of these characters and what unifies them. It's fun. We get to write for Ginnifer [Goodwin] as both Snow White and Mary Margaret. We get to explore different parts of the same character.'

They were clearly going to have fun with their new creation. 'I think this is the first time anyone's ever shown Snow White (*Big Love*'s Ginnifer Goodwin) swinging a sword – and she's pregnant! – and ABC was cool with that,' said Kitsis in an interview with *tvline.com*. To those in the know, there were also plenty of references to *Lost*. Regina's house number is 108, a number that frequently occurred in *Lost*. For example, the Oceanic Six left the island after 108 days and the button in the hatch had to be pressed every 108 minutes. The town clock is stuck at 8.15, the same number as the doomed *Lost* flight. Emma has a car sticker for Geronimo Jackson, a 1970s rock band sometimes mentioned on *Lost*. The smoke monster engulfs the Enchanted Forest, another entity encountered in *Lost*. 'Damon [Lindelof, *Lost* co-creator] has been a godfather to us,' said Kitsis to *tvline.com*. 'His name is not on the show, but he is in the DNA of it.'

They had any number of other cultural references to plunder as well. There were the actual characters themselves, of course, taken from numerous fairy tales, and so the viewers heard Leroy, who is really the dwarf Grumpy, whistling 'Heigh-Ho', which is what the dwarves sang in the 1937 version of Disney's *Snow White and the Seven Dwarves*. To further highlight the link, the production company behind the new show was ABC Studios, a subsidiary of Disney, which was handy, as Disney allowed them access to their fairy tales for use in the series, and didn't object to Snow White being pregnant. There was another Disney reference when Emma wishes on a blue star candle, as Pinocchio did in the 1940 film of the same name, where his wish is granted by the Blue Fairy, who makes an appearance with Jiminy Cricket. Then there was the wardrobe, which Snow White and Prince Charming use to transport their new-born baby to a different universe, a clear reference to the magical wardrobe used in *The Lion, The Witch and the Wardrobe* to transport the characters to Narnia.

All in all, it was a staggeringly original project from some of the best minds in the business, and on the whole the critics loved it. 'No other new show this fall is attempting to tell a bigger story, and we're hoping the rough patches smooth out and it fulfills the potential that's there in its very strong cast and premise,' said Rick Porter of *Zap2it*, mentioning Jennifer Morrison (Emma Swan) and Jared Gilmore's (Emma's ten-year-old son Henry) performances when they appear in scenes together. 'As such it falls to Morrison to move the story along in this world, and fortunately for the audience she's able to pull it off. She gives a confident, grounded performance that helps keep the show from feeling too fantastical, and her rapport with Gilmore is a big plus too . . . Given the cast and the people involved behind the scenes . . . we're more optimistic than not that *Once Upon a Time* will find its way. But if it doesn't, at least it will go down swinging.'

Mike Hale in the *New York Times* compared *Once Upon a Time* with the series Grimm, with which it had some similarities, but said the former has a 'richer premise and more interesting characters'. He liked Ginnifer Goodwin's (Snow White) and Morrison's performances, but sounded a slightly duff note: 'Watching the pilot again, though, it became harder to ignore the soap opera underpinnings and the twee sentimentality.' Well, it was supposed to be a fairy tale, after all.

Amy Ratcliffe of *IGN* gave the episode an 8/10 and liked the casting, acting and writing, despite 'a few cheesy' moments, saying she hoped the series would remain focused on its story rather than on too many special effects.

Christine Orlando of *TV Fanatic* loved it, giving the episode 4.4 out of 5 stars, calling it 'a beautiful, stunning, magical journey . . . [I was] hooked from the opening scene.' She liked everyone, particularly Carlyle, saying he made a 'perfectly creepy Rumpelstiltskin'. Of Henry she said, 'He's spunky, intelligent and has just the right amount of persistence and faith in fantasy to make you want to believe . . . Very, very good.'

In all it was a triumph and one that would finally send Jamie on his way.

7

The Heart Is a Lonely Hunter

Jamie's part in *Once Upon a Time* was mainly limited to series one, where it was a fairly pivotal role. In fairyland, in the tradition of so many fairy tales, he was the nameless Hunter, raised by wolves, with whom he forms a deep and lasting bond. He too was a reference to a Disney original as Humbert, his human name, is the name of the Hunter in *Snow White and the Seven Dwarves*.

Strangely enough, however, the character was initially conceived as someone else altogether, namely a famous fictional detective. 'Here's something interesting,' said Kitsis to *E! Online*. 'Originally the sheriff was Sherlock Holmes. He was going to be a detective and his curse was that he was in a town with no mystery. So he was this bored sheriff. There was a rights issue so we couldn't get it . . . but now we're so in love with the BBC's Sherlock, I don't want to even play in that arena. We'll never have Sherlock unless Benedict Cumberbatch wants to come on.' So the Hunter Jamie was. Funnily enough, when he auditioned for *The Fall* a couple of years later, he originally auditioned to be a policeman, before landing the much bigger part of Paul Spector.

When the part in *Once Upon a Time* came up, Jamie knew immediately that he wanted to do it. He was getting places with his acting now and had started to realize there was a lot of dross out there, so when something good came along it was wise to snap it up. 'Look, I was just going through pilot season, and you know, you read so much shit,' he told *E! Online*. 'So much of it is repetitive and you've seen that show a thousand times. You get sort of tired of hearing about it. *Once Upon a Time* really stood out. It was the show that everyone was talking about, that all my agents were going mad over and that seemed like a definite go.' It was also an extremely original concept, not always a given in an industry that works out what has been successful and then produces endless variations on the same theme.

Jamie was also exceedingly keen to work with Horowitz and Kitsis. 'The chances are that if they're involved in something, it's going to be something that you're going to want to be involved in,' he said. 'I was such a fan of *Lost*, so they didn't have to explain who they were. You get involved like any other TV show and just hope. But it was the one that I thought, This is different and this will grab people, because there's no one in the world that doesn't like fairy tales.' It sounded very much as if Jamie was hoping for long-term involvement in the show, although he later said he knew what would happen to his character right from the start. Nevertheless it was heady stuff: high-profile prime-time American television. It was a huge opportunity and he was determined to make it work.

Initially the audience wasn't told who the Sheriff's fairy-tale counterpart was. 'It's a cool way to keep the audience guessing and to be the source of that sort of wonder is quite cool,' said Jamie. 'I think fans will be a bit pleased that he is something a little bit different and controversial.' It also gave him a somewhat mythic quality as details were deliberately kept vague.

Jamie had been thinking about the back story to his character, the points of interest for viewers, and as he did with so many of his characters, he'd thought the role through. What about his relationship with Emma, which upsets matters somewhat with Regina, with whom he has been having a relationship? 'I think it's real,' said Jamie. 'I think he relates to her on a different level than he has related to anyone else. Everyone else is kind of stuck in that time, and every time he talks to her [he wants to] know more. He's genuinely attracted to her. Emma is the first person to come along that has made him start to question his relationship with Regina, and he's actually starting to [ask himself] what drives him to it . . . He just wants to feel something, and Emma is his opportunity to do that.'

And what about the relationship with Regina? 'I think in Storybrooke you're not really spoilt for choice when it comes to relationships,' said Jamie, sounding – just for once – not as tactful as he could have been when talking about his on-screen love interest. Perhaps he'd got fed up with answering questions about it. 'You sort of take what you can get. You know, the mayor is single, she's attractive and she's powerful.'

She was also the pivotal point of the story and as such it upped Jamie's profile to play her on-screen amour.

The story goes that, in fairyland, evil Queen Regina thinks Jamie, as the Hunter, would be just the chap to kill Snow White and so she hires him as an assassin. In the event, however, the Hunter cannot bring himself to do it and hands over a stag's heart instead of Snow White's. Evil Regina takes this rather badly and tears out the Hunter's heart, which she stashes in her vault, effectively making him her slave. He then proceeds to save the life of Prince Charming, assisting his escape, but refusing offers of help himself, saying that the sacrifice of his heart must not be in vain.

Jamie appeared to be loving the way the show was going. 'Episode two there's a lot happening with Regina, because like *Lost* . . . in the early stages everyone has their own episode pretty much,' he told *E! Online*. 'And you get a better taste of their background and what's brought them to this point. The second episode concentrates on Regina and the Evil Queen, so it's exciting. I have some fun stuff. We'll see the mayor start to crumble a little bit. It's so layered and clever beyond belief. It's meticulous in how it's thought up. Every single thing that happens, there's a reason for it, and it corresponds to something that happened in fairy-tale land. It's pretty complex stuff, but it's fun . . . I can't reveal too much about mine [his character in fairyland]. Essentially they're the same person at their core . . . It's a pretty big challenge . . . but that's the fun of it. One day you're just being normal, and then the next, you're in fairy-tale land. It's crazy. It's cool.'

Over in Storybrooke, Jamie's character was Sheriff Graham Humbert, the lawmaker in town. In the early episodes he assists evil Regina, with whom he is secretly involved, helping her to stop Owen and Kurt Flynn from leaving town, but when Emma Swan arrives on the scene things change. He begins to recover his memories, but is faintly bemused to discover that he doesn't appear to have a heart, prompting him to finish his relationship with Regina. He then becomes involved with Emma and fully recovers his memory, at which point evil Regina crushes his heart and, somewhat to the shock of at least part of the audience, he dies. How could they? The handsome Hunter? What would this do for Jamie's chances of establishing a successful career in the States?

Jamie assured fans that right from the outset he had known his character would be killed off and that it had not come as a shock to him. 'I did know,' he told *E! Entertainment* in the immediate aftermath of the plot twist. Whether or not he was telling the truth, he certainly sounded sad that the experience had come to an end. 'I knew when we started shooting for real. It makes it a quite odd experience because, obviously, I do feel a part of that family. I've been there since day one; the pilot and then the whole waiting for the series to get picked up. All through that, I didn't know at that stage, to be honest. Yeah, it came as a bit of a shock to me at the start, but then we still had all these episodes to shoot, so I definitely still wanted to be involved in the show . . .'

Jamie was sounding more wistful by the second and was also learning another truism of show business: that you make friends with the people you work with and then, when the work is over, that's that. You have to move on. It can be difficult to do this, all the more so when it's a long-running show in which you thought you would be playing a long-running part.

'It was a strange thing because I've seriously bonded with these people,' he continued. 'We're all stuck together for four months and you make proper friendships. The weird thing always weighing in the back of my mind was the final episode was getting closer and closer. You start trying to adjust accordingly. I'm not sure if this will be the last you'll ever see of my face on the show, but it's certainly the last you'll see of Sheriff Graham.'

But could there be a way back? His fairy-tale character hadn't actually died, he pointed out, which meant that it was entirely possible he would return to the show in some format, something he clearly wanted to do. Whatever the case, the death of Sheriff Graham was a huge talking point, and if nothing else it made Jamie the focus of a great deal of attention. Not only was his character disposed of, but the manner of his death was fairly unusual too. 'It's pretty gruesome, but you know, it's a little bit cool,' said Jamie, a man who had appeared in a zombie flick and thus knew a gruesome death when he saw one. 'Not many people get to die like that. It's a bit cooler than getting shot in the arse or something. So as TV deaths go, I was pretty happy.' He also pointed out that killing off a popular character was a way of illustrating that the curse was deadly serious.

Jamie's profile had received a massive boost and he had really proved he could act – a fact that had never been doubted by the people who had seen him perform, though his series of short films hadn't had a massive audience, while his appearance in the more well-known *Marie Antoinette* had only been a short one. As a result, he was still best known for being the model who had once dated Keira Knightley, a fact he was coming to resent more and more. Having bowed out of the series, it was slightly unclear what he would do next. Would he go back to full-time modelling? Would he manage to land another role on prime-time television? And would he finally manage to shake the misapprehension that he was nothing more than a pretty face?

Jamie put a brave face on it, but there was evidence that he wished he hadn't had to leave the show quite so soon. He joked about arriving back in London 'five years early', and further revealed that he'd stopped using Twitter so much because he didn't want to give anything away about what was happening in the series. Meanwhile there were more mixed messages from those involved in the film: would Jamie return in some way in the second series? Initially, Ed Kitsis wasn't keen: 'If we brought him back, everyone would say we were messing with continuity,' he said. 'We don't want to do that.' But it was clear that everyone had been taken aback by the backlash from Jamie's fans, who wanted him back in the series. What could be done?

Rumours of Jamie's unhappiness refused to go away. 'Jamie is best known for dating an English rose,' one source told the

Daily Mirror. 'But he wants to be known for something more than being Keira Knightley's arm candy. He had built up a big following on *Once Upon a Time* and it's a bitter pill for him to swallow.' Ironically, Jamie's star was shortly to rise so high and so quickly that although the makers of *Once Upon a Time* would have loved to have him back, it would be too late.

He did return to the show briefly, though, in season two, in an episode entitled 'Welcome to Storybrooke', which took place twenty-eight years earlier, on the first day of the curse. Jamie was clearly enjoying himself and glad to be back among his friends in the series that had boosted his profile so much. 'Storybrooke is pretty much almost identical to how we see it up to this point,' he told *hollywoodreporter.com*. 'It's the first day of the curse, so essentially nothing really changes from that point onwards. There are a few references to the fact that it's twenty years before [the start of the series]. The [producers] have been quite clever with putting in some music that's on in the background at Granny's, which lets the audience know that we're dealing with a different time. It's fascinating to see, from the first day of the curse, Regina had total control – especially over Graham.'

In this episode, viewers are shown the beginning of the great romance that was to end so unfortunately, and once again Jamie was keen to elaborate. 'In season one, we see the fact that she's in control of him, to a point, and getting what she wants from him,' said Jamie. '[In this episode] we get to see it right from the start. We can see the scale of it, how easily she can get him to do what she wants. It's kind of sad. It's kind of tragic – to see someone get used, essentially, like a puppet. We see her at her most evil and controlling. Poor Graham, he's just doing what he's told. He doesn't have the conscience to fight against it. It's kind of hard to watch. I find myself feeling very sorry for him. It's interesting, I think, for the audience to see the level of manipulation from day one of the curse.'

He appeared to be enjoying inhabiting the character again. 'It was almost two years ago to the day that we were filming the pilot,' he continued. 'I got to know those people extremely well. I very much feel like I'm part of the makeup of *Once Upon a Time*. It didn't feel that weird going back; it felt normal. In a lovely way, you slide back in. I loved it. It's kind of bizarre to hang that leather jacket up and think that that's the last time you'll be wearing it, and then, lo and behold, you're back in. It's really sweet. I'm happy to be involved.' In a way, it had allowed him to say goodbye to the character and that particular stage of his career in a more gentle fashion. And it also reassured Jamie that there was a way in which his character could return to the series, even if it was only via flashbacks to the past.

In a clear sign of his popularity, he was told that some of the fans had kept his character alive. 'That's nice,' said Jamie bashfully. 'Love from the fans is flattering. That's what makes the show. They are so essential to everything involved with *Once Upon a Time*. If I have them on my side, that can only be a good thing. I'm not going to take all the credit; Graham's a well-written and interesting character. The reaction to Graham's death . . . I'm pleased that people are so concerned, but [joking] I don't think we need to be calling the FBI or anything.'

Jamie had always had fans, from his early days modelling, but now, for the first time, he was beginning to attract the attention more usually reserved for big stars. It started gradually and then, every time it was announced that he had landed another big role, there was a big jump in fan numbers. Jamie, however, had seen Keira swamped by fans, and as a result he was pretty cautious. Nevertheless, it went with the territory and he would have to learn how to cope.

After *Once Upon a Time* finished he returned to modelling – with such a lucrative career why would he stop? Eyebrows nearly hit the ceiling, however, when he appeared in another Calvin Klein campaign, this time struggling, half naked, with a Russian supermodel. It provoked uproar in some cases, something Jamie responded to pretty coolly. 'Calvin Klein wants to be controversial, so if people are demonstrating under a billboard of me getting my arse bitten by Natalia Vodianova, then that's a win for them, because it creates attention,' he said. 'I hope that's the closest I'll ever come to porn.' Anyway, he was used to it – a similar furore had broken out when he had been pictured a few years earlier with Eva Mendes.

For that was another complicating factor in Jamie's life: although he frequently played down his modelling career, saying that it wasn't important, it was so lucrative that part of him didn't want to give it up. Yes, he wanted to be taken seriously as an actor, yes he was fed up with being described as 'arm candy' (especially when the words Keira and Knightley were involved) and yes he wanted to be considered a man of substance. But when a seriously lucrative advertising campaign lands in your lap, you think twice before turning it down. And so Jamie continued modelling whilst pursuing his burgeoning acting career.

Although the endless speculation about his love life continued, behind the scenes a very different story was playing out. Jamie had been hinting for some time now that he had been dating and was in a relationship, although it was still in the early stages. Before it was clear whether or not it would go the distance, he wasn't inclined to name names. However, things were getting serious now and so it finally emerged that he had a steady girlfriend, Amelia Warner, a singer/songwriter signed to Island Records, who performed under the name of Slow Moving Millie, a name given to her by her friends because she took so long to get her music career going. And it was she who was to become Mrs Dornan, much to the chagrin of Jamie's fans.

8

Slow Moving Millie

Amelia Catherine Bennett was born on 4 June 1982 on Merseyside to a theatrical family: her parents Annette Ekblom and Alun Lewis were both actors and so is her uncle Hywel Bennett. When she was four years old she moved with her mother to London after her parents divorced and attended the Royal Masonic School for Girls, followed by the College of Fine Arts. Like Jamie, she was interested in acting from an early age. After devising and acting out a play with friends in London's Covent Garden, she was spotted by a talent scout, after which she joined the Royal Court Youth Theatre.

With her dark brown hair and gamine features, there is a slight physical resemblance to Keira, and like Keira, she has a strong personality. 'I've got this idea that who you play in the nativity relates to who you are in life,' she once told the *Guardian*. 'When I was four, I was Mary. But I wasn't a lovely ethereal Mary, I was a right bossy cow. I stopped the play in the middle to tell Joseph he was doing it all wrong. So that's me . . . And I've got this best friend who was so bitter about never being Mary. And everyone else, everyone you meet, always says, "Oh, I was the Angel Gabriel. The Messenger." Never Mary or Joseph . . . Have you noticed? So yeah, who you are in the nativity, it determines, you know, your . . .'

Early roles were in *Kavanagh QC* (her first role), *Casualty*, *Aristocrats*, *Mansfield Park* and *Don Quixote*, and then she landed the part of Jodie Whitemore, a kidnap victim, in *Waking the Dead*. Amelia was not just a pretty face: having achieved two As and a B at A level, she had a place to read history of art at Goldsmiths College, but decided instead to concentrate on her acting career. She also appeared in an adaptation of Kingsley Amis's *Take a Girl Like You*, about the womanizing teacher Patrick Standish, where she garnered criticism on the grounds that she was too pretty for the role. 'Last night, it was the turn of Sheila, the jail-bait daughter of Patrick Standish's headmaster. As Patrick himself commented, her main qualifications for sexual attention were that "she was there and she was willing". But the viewer can't have helped noticing that, as played by Amelia Warner, she was also rather cute, a fact which tended to spoil the dramatic point – Patrick is so weak-willed and cheap that he will shag any woman at all, no matter how unattractive.'

Things really began to look up when she starred in the 2000 BBC two-part adaptation of *Lorna Doone* in the title role. The story is of a star-crossed couple, Lorna and a working farmer called John Ridd, played by Richard Coyle, who lived with his family on Exmoor. He feuds with the aristocratic outlaw Doones before falling for the beautiful Lorna, who is in fact engaged to her cousin, the rotter Carver Doone.

Much drama ensues, and it was to become the highlight of Christmas television viewing that year, also starring such big names as Aidan Gillen as Carver, Martin Jarvis, Barbara Flynn and Michael Kitchen.

Amelia went on to feature in *Quills*, in which she played Simone, the schoolgirl wife of the Marquis de Sade's physician Dr Royer-Collard, played by Michael Caine. The film was about the last days of the Marquis; set in an asylum, it starred Geoffrey Rush and Kate Winslet and created quite a stir: Amelia was only seventeen at the time – she wasn't legally allowed to see the film until she was eighteen – and despite her relative youth, she displayed a maturity beyond her years and was beginning to be spoken of as the next big thing. 'I think it was harder for him to be honest,' she said to the *Mail on Sunday*, talking about her co-star Michael Caine, who essentially had to attack his child bride. 'I just had to lie there and look pained and upset, which was easy because it was awful. It was more difficult for him because even his youngest daughter is older than me.'

Michael Caine was obviously a legend in the acting profession, but Amelia was unfazed. 'When I started making *Quills* I only knew him from *Jaws 4*,' she told *The Times*. 'I was a lot more impressed about the prospect of working with Kate Winslet, to be honest. Then my friends told me what a legend he was and got me to watch videos of *Get Carter*, *Hannah and Her Sisters* and *The Italian Job*. It was fascinating to watch him working. He comes across as being a very straightforward actor, but you're aware that there's a lot going on in his head. He really looked after me in a paternal way. Some of the scenes we had to do were horrible, especially for him as a father, but he made them as nice as they could have been for me.'

The film on the whole garnered fairly good reviews. 'There's trouble down at the asylum,' wrote Henry Fitzherbert in the *Sunday Express*. 'The inmates can't keep their hands to themselves, the laundry maid reads dirty stories to the staff and the priest has a stirring in his cassock. It's *Carry On Marquis*, the story of the Marquis De Sade, that devilish French aristocrat who spent the last decade of his life locked up with a bunch of madmen.'

The *Daily Record*, however, was not quite so impressed. 'He's been called a depraved freak, a sex-obsessed fiend and, in every sense, a rotten writer,' it said in the review. 'But crude and cruel as he was, maybe even the Marquis De Sade doesn't deserve a biography that goes so completely over the top as Quills . . . The hateful Royer-Collard is a bigger sadist than Sade – and unlike the Marquis, his nasty acts are not limited to his imagination. On his way to the asylum, Royer-Collard picks up a child bride (Amelia Warner) and locks her up in his renovated castle, where he expects her total obedience.' It may have been in the wake of a rather searing role, but Amelia was certainly getting noticed.

Shortly afterwards, it was announced that Amelia, who seemed set to become a major star at this point, would present a prize at the *Evening Standard* British Film Awards. Then she was swept off to Los Angeles, a city she grew to dislike, but which, in those early heady days, appeared to be a dream come true. 'I had a great time,' she told *The Times*. 'The first week was silly, just getting used to the whole Hollywood thing – piles of clothes sent to you, cars to take you out to dinner – it was a laugh. I know people say LA is superficial, but I found the people lovely and laid back, and their drive and ambition exciting . . . I was approached about some new films, but I don't want to do typical popcorn teen-comedy stuff.'

'I want to stay below the radar and make good films,' she told the *Guardian*. 'I have to be careful, I don't want my life to change. I really don't want to be a movie star. I cringe when people are like . . . I am going to be an actress! Which is really probably quite mean of me. But it would have made me uncomfortable to actually think or say I wanted to do it . . . so I didn't. I fell into it, really. And then, once I was in it, I thought I'd try, at least give it a go, and see how it went.' In that sense, she was unlike Jamie, who had been quite clear that he wanted to be an actor from the start, but like Jamie she was wary of the down side of celebrity. And there was a good reason for that.

Like Jamie, she had experience of what it was like to date a significantly more famous other half. In her case it was the actor Colin Farrell, whom she met in LA. It was only a brief relationship, lasting about a year, but it was quite serious. After the two became an item, they were seen in each other's company all the time and created quite a stir. Colin was on the brink of a major Hollywood career, and as such attracted a good deal of attention; while Amelia, fresh from her *Lorna Doone* and *Quills* triumphs, was being tipped for great things herself. Briefly, they were a very hot Hollywood couple, both on a personal and professional note.

'We met just before *Quills* came out and I can tell you the exact moment I fell in love with her,' Colin, who was by now being referred to as the 'Irish Brad Pitt' told the *Daily Express* after they split up. 'She's beautiful. It was at the premiere, on the red carpet, and I stepped back because it wasn't my night. It was hers. She steps forward, looks at all the lights and cameras, then looks back at me with this killer help-me look on her face. She reached out for me and that was it. Right through the heart . . . Too fast. Too young.' Amelia also talked about the fact that they were simply too young to make it work.

Even so, in August 2001, there was a sense of shock when it turned out that the couple – Amelia was now nineteen and Colin twenty-five – had suddenly tied the knot. The two were holidaying on some islands in the Pacific and took the decision pretty much on the spur of the moment: 'We went to Bora Bora in French Polynesia and just got the local priest to take us out on an island,' Colin told the *Mirror*. They certainly made a handsome couple and Amelia's mother Annette was delighted. 'It's great they've found each other,' she told the *Mirror*. 'I love him and it's a relief for me that Millie's met someone who looks after her and who she can trust. It's rare that they're both young but so ready to commit. And she didn't have to kiss many frogs before she found her prince!' She might have spoken a little too soon.

Colin was shooting up the Hollywood A list, now entering the league where he could command millions per film. But he was also garnering a reputation for wildness, not hesitating to use bad language in interviews and looking a little young to be settling down. Nevertheless, it was a shock when, in February 2002, after just six months of marriage, it turned out the couple had split up. Colin denied that either his career or anyone else had anything to do with it. 'I'm sure there are some relationships that can't sustain the demands of being an actor,' he told the *Sunday Mirror*, 'but that didn't play any role in the marriage at all. That didn't happen and I'm not seeing anyone romantically at the moment either.'

Neither particularly wanted to talk about it but the truth is that both were devastated. They might not have been a couple for long, but it had been a very intense relationship and it took both of them a while before they were ready to move on. Colin told the *Mirror*, 'It's all over and done with. Been there and back. I'm heading straight for a sabbatical. I think it's the priesthood for me.'

There was nothing for it but to get a divorce. But then it turned out that wasn't necessary, as they had never been legally married in the first place. It seemed neither knew that was the case, and both were taken aback to hear it, although it must be said that in more recent years, Amelia has been keen to play down this somewhat embarrassing episode in her life.

'We didn't actually get married – it's not actually true,' she told the *Sun* years later. 'I think we've been too polite to deny it. We had a ceremony on a beach in Tahiti that was by no means legal and we knew it wasn't. It was just a thing we did on holiday . . . It really wasn't this secret wedding that no one was invited to. It was lovely, it was silly, it was sweet, but by no means was it a serious thing and I think my mum thought it was quite funny . . . It was a very intense and passionate relationship. It was heartbreaking when it ended.'

By the mid-2000s, Amelia's acting career began to slow down. Like so many people tipped to be the next big thing, it never quite happened, despite the fact that she was talented and beautiful, and Amelia now began to experience one of the serious downsides of celebrity, when your career isn't going according to plan. The work might have tailed off, but her name was still constantly mentioned in the press, owing to her relationship with Colin. Every time he got a new girlfriend, which was frequently at that stage, Amelia's name came up, complete with the details of their four-month 'marriage', as it did when another girlfriend of his got pregnant. By this time he had a reputation as something of a wild man and so the papers were full of his exploits, which couldn't have been easy for Amelia. Just as Jamie spent years being spoken of as Keira's ex, so Amelia was having to put up with the same apropos Colin, who constantly appeared on lists of hot Hollywood actors and was even being called a sex addict. It was all a far cry from that beach in Tahiti.

'The Colin I knew was very different from the Colin I see now,' she told the *Sunday Mirror* as his latest exploits dominated the headlines. 'That's why I feel I can't talk about our relationship, because it's as if I'm talking about a different person. It kind of upsets me to see how he's being represented now – or how he chooses to represent himself to play that part.'

When Colin was linked to Britney Spears, 'friends' of Amelia quoted her as saying he would never settle down. That was as maybe, but Amelia had clearly meant more to him than his lengthening stream of conquests. 'We fell in love very hard, we married and we fell out of love equally as hard,' he told the *Daily Star*. 'It was that simple and that complicated and that flippant and that spontaneous. The two of us wanted to go on holiday and we wanted to get hitched. We thought, Let's kill two birds with one stone. Instead of going to the Elvis chapel, let's f*** off to the beach and get married in Tahiti. And we had a great time. Right or wrong, it's for nobody to decide but me. I was the one that did it and I'd do it all over again through the tears.'

Amelia clearly felt pretty much the same. 'We were in Tahiti. We went to the activities desk and said, "We want to go jet-skiing and shark-feeding and . . . we want to get married,"' she said in an interview with the *Sunday Mirror* in 2004. 'They said, "Cool, we'll do the shark-feeding on Monday, jet-skiing on Tuesday and we can fit in a wedding on Wednesday." It wasn't legally binding, it was just something we did for us. I loved him so much and I had the most amazing times of my life with him. He was a fantastic partner. We were together just over a year and we spent just two days apart that whole time. We were just living in each other's pockets. He didn't do anything wrong, we were just too young. I had stuff to do and he had stuff to do and it just didn't work out, which was really sad.'

Meanwhile, Amelia's career continued, although on a much lesser scale to Colin's. There were a few more film roles, although nothing like the glory days of the year 2000. Then in 2002, she was in a rather idiotic horror film called *Nine Lives*, notable mainly because it starred Paris Hilton, about a group of friends who spend the weekend in a country house in Scotland and die, one by one. That was followed by a romantic comedy called *Love's Brother* in 2003; *Winter Passing*, which at least starred some bona-fide Hollywood names such as Will Ferrell and Ed Harris, though it met with a decidedly mixed reception; *Aeon Flux*, a science fiction outing; *Stoned*, a film about the Rolling Stone Brian Jones who died in the late 1960s in mysterious circumstances; *Alpha Male* and *Gone*, a psychological thriller in the Australian outback, which garnered some pretty good reviews. 'Another British film, *Gone*, is a striking psychological thriller set against the photogenic backdrop of the Australian outback. Alex (Shaun Evans) and Sophie (Amelia Warner) play the British couple backpacking their way into trouble in the company of a charismatic American loner, Taylor (Scott Mechlowicz),' wrote Wendy Ide in *The Times*. 'You may be able to work out where it's going, but it's an enjoyable ride nonetheless.'

'The couple, having taken up the American's offer of a lift, gradually discover that Taylor might be more than just a cuckoo in the nest,' said Anthony Quinn in the *Independent*. 'Director Ringan Ledwidge relies too heavily in the early scenes on poppy montages, but once the trio reaches the outback and the sexual tension mounts he suddenly tightens the noose to leave us fighting for breath. Gone, but not forgotten.' Other reviews were also pretty positive, but for whatever reason, it didn't manage to revive Amelia's film career.

Then there was *The Seeker* and *The Echo*. Neither set the world alight and neither put her in the spotlight as she had once been. Meanwhile, she was becoming disillusioned; something was bound to give.

What gave was acting, with Amelia deciding to give it up altogether and start a full-time career as a musician instead. 'It [acting] wasn't fulfilling,' she told the *Daily Telegraph*. 'You have no control, there is no responsibility, you go to the audition, and you either get the part or you don't – that's as much choice as you have. Then a year later you see the end product and you can be in a completely different film from the one you thought you were making. It started to get really frustrating. At least with music, you can write a song and it exists in the world, even if no one hears it. That's lovely.'

With music Amelia had some success. She composed some film soundtracks, put out an independent EP and landed a contract with Island records, partly on the back of one song, 'Beasts', which had been used in a Virgin Media advert. She recorded an album, *Renditions*, which was a series of covers of 1980s hits from the likes of Bananarama, the Thompson Twins and Yahoo. 'I think Eighties music can get a bad rap because of the naff way it was produced,' she told the *Independent*. 'The lyrics are really dark, but are trussed up in these manic assaults of melody and sound. But underneath they're actually really poignant songs, and they're all about having your heart broken.'

But it was another cover version that really grabbed people's attention in 2011. Morrissey once recorded a number called 'Please, Please, Please Let Me Get What I Want', and Amelia sang a cover version, which was used by John Lewis in a £6 million Christmas ad campaign. Some Morrissey fans were enraged, but the man himself was, by all accounts, rather pleased with the version.

'It wasn't a long and difficult road actually. It was relatively straightforward getting the rights,' said John Lewis director of marketing Craig Inglis. 'We approached the record company and Morrissey back in July, and they gave their approval. It is an iconic track from an iconic British band. We know our audience holds the Smiths and bands from that era in high esteem.'

It was then that Amelia met Jamie, though, given that the two inhabited the same rarefied entertainment world, Amelia had by then developed a healthy suspicion of LA, or at least an unfortunate take on it, and really loathed Hollywood. She wasn't afraid to say so, either: 'I don't even really want to talk about how I hate LA. It's so English to hate LA,' she told the *Guardian*, in marked contrast to an earlier interview she'd given. 'I'd like to say I love it, but I don't. It's such a weird place. If it were my choice, I wouldn't spend a day there.

Everything shuts at eleven. And everyone thinks they're so crazy and wild and liberal and they're not!'

Her acting career was well and truly in the past now. She was a musician, not an actress, and she was very happy to talk about her change of career. 'The constant pressure of having to prove myself as an actress didn't sit well with me. I got fed up with acting because my heart was never in it. I'd be in LA auditioning in front of thirty people,' she told the *Independent*. 'The feedback I always got was that I didn't want it. I was up against lots of actresses who would fight tooth and nail for a part but I didn't have the passion. I didn't want to suffer through the moments of nervousness. I felt exposed and judged all the time. So I thought it was best to get out. Music is my soulmate but that's what stopped me from doing it for so long. I felt like if I get judged on this that would be devastating. But at least I have the passion to get through it.'

She was certainly going to be exposed again soon, however, by virtue of who she was marrying. Like Jamie, Amelia was about to take a step into the unknown, although in her case it was as a result of the man she was to marry rather than what she did with her career. Simply by virtue of being Mrs Dornan, she was about to step into the full glare of the spotlight, her every move examined; her every activity scrutinized, but she didn't have quite the take-no-prisoners attitude of the most successful Hollywood stars. 'I'm ambitious, but not competitive,' she once said. 'You'd drive yourself crazy if you were. You know, there are actually enough jobs out there for all of us.' It was certainly an admirable philosophy and one that set her out as a decent human being, but it showed that her priorities were different from a lot of the people she mixed with.

As far as her relationship was concerned, however, this was a plus. For years now Jamie had made no secret of the fact that he wanted to be a major star, but there tends to be room for only one person with such overwhelming ambition in a relationship, so it was all to the good that Amelia was prepared to take a step back. That, perhaps, was another of the reasons for his split with Keira – young as he was when it happened, Jamie might have realized that the two of them could have ended up competing, which can't be good for a relationship. Strangely enough, Keira might have felt the same way, possibly without realizing it, for when she got married (in the same year as Jamie), it was also to a musician, James Righton, rather than to a fellow actor. Both she and Jamie went on to choose people who were their equals and who could stand up to them, but who didn't compete in the same arena.

This was just as well, for Jamie, despite the uncertainty caused by leaving *Once Upon a Time*, was about to take on a role that would be the making of him. And it certainly didn't rely on him being just a pretty face.

9

No One Knows What's Going on Inside Someone Else's Head

J amie was now on the international radar in a way he'd never been before. He may or may not have been unhappy about leaving *Once Upon a Time*, but the fact was that the show had increased his profile dramatically and brought him to the attention of casting directors who might otherwise have been unaware of him. This was about to be demonstrated to spectacular effect in a role that totally transformed the public's perception of him, illustrating that he had outstanding talent as an actor and was able to take on truly disturbing and memorable roles. For Jamie had won the part of Paul Spector, a brutally sadistic serial killer who is also a caring family man.

It's often been observed that Jamie brings a kind of silent intensity to his roles on screen and that this might be due to growing up during the Troubles in Belfast. *The Fall*, Jamie's latest series, was set in Belfast, although the brooding air of mystery and terror were based on something very different, a crazed psychopath who could hardly have seemed more normal at first glance. The premise was this: Gillian Anderson (who got top billing) was Stella Gibson, a Detective

Superintendent from London's Met, who is drafted in to help the police force in Belfast solve a mysterious killing. She quickly identifies similarities with another murder and, rather more quickly than anyone else, realizes there is a serial killer on the loose.

Unusually for a series like this, the audience knows who the killer is from the start. Paul Spector is a bereavement counsellor who is married with two small children, to whom he is a clearly devoted father, playing with the two of them, watching his little daughter dance and generally giving the impression of being a contented family man. He also volunteers with the Samaritans at night, though this ends up being a cover for what he's really getting up to. For Paul is actually a monster, stalking his victims and plotting what he will do to them in a notebook that he keeps hidden in a loft from which his daughter's mobile dangles, before carrying out the act. The brilliantly plotted and suspenseful episodes were based around the fact that there were two hunters at work: Paul, on the lookout for more victims, and Stella, who was hunting him. The juxtaposition of caring young father with brutal killer was enormously striking – and it couldn't be further from those Calvin Klein ads either.

Jamie appeared topless early on in the series, but there was pretty stiff competition on the torso front from some of his fellow male actors, in particular one police officer, James Olsen, whom Stella bedded early on in the series. Stella's blouses, worn unbuttoned racily low, also became a major talking point, not to mention a part of the plot when they burst open rather inappropriately at a murder investigation press conference. The show was brilliantly atmospheric and totally compelling – a tour de force for everyone involved.

It was also a new departure for Jamie, who seemed at pains to apologize for the terrible actions of the character he played on screen, whilst pointing out the massive difference between himself and the part he played. 'I don't think it would have been too good for me to stay in that head space for three months,' he told the *Daily Mirror*. 'When it was appropriate, I would make someone laugh. There were scenes where I've got a ligature around my victim's neck and I'm pretending to squeeze with all my life. She's foaming at the mouth, my sweat's dripping in her eyes, I'm watching her die and her eyes are bulging. After every one of those scenes, when they'd say, "Cut!" I was saying, "Oh my God I'm so sorry. I'm going to untie your feet here. Is that OK?" Because I am not that guy. I did my best to slip out of it as soon as "cut" was called. You don't want to be in that head space all the time. Certain actors would but I remember thinking I was in over my head when they cast me.'

In fact, the casting had been inspired. This was a world away from his role as the handsome Hunter and his image as a model who wanted to break into acting. It showed he had depth, could play dark, multi-dimensional characters and delve into the psyche of a terrible mind. In short, it showed he wasn't just another pretty boy, and that, potentially, a serious acting career lay ahead. It also demonstrated a healthy attitude towards his new profession: unlike some method actors, who think they have to stay in the role full time, Jamie was perfectly able to step away from it when the day's filming was done. It spoke of an inner security that was clearly a product of his close relationship with his family and of a happy relationship with his new wife.

Despite this, he had to find a way to get inside Spector's head, and he did this by watching videos of the American serial killer Ted Bundy. Bundy was a monster; a rapist, kidnapper and necrophile, he was also handsome and charismatic, which is how he lured so many victims to their fate. He was at large in the US throughout the 1970s, and possibly earlier, and would return to the bodies of his victims, grooming them in death (a trait he and Spector share) until he was finally arrested in 1975. He managed to escape and commit more crimes until he was rearrested in 1978; after years spent denying what he had done he finally admitted to thirty murders between 1974 and 1978, although the true figure could have been much higher. In 1989 he was executed in the electric chair.

He was exactly the sort of murderous psychopath Jamie was being called upon to portray, and Jamie took his research seriously, trying to understand the machinations of a mind the vast majority of people could not possibly understand. 'I read a lot about serial killers,' Jamie told *PA*. 'I think a lot of these guys have things in common, whether it's abuse or abandonment. I read a lot of books, about Bundy especially. I watched every interview. He was the most fascinating serial killer because he was a professional and he was good-looking.

He was a charming guy. Also, he had a girlfriend for seven years who never suspected, even when he was killing a woman a month. That is terrifying, that there is someone like this who can go unnoticed in society and lead a normal life but carry out these unspeakable acts. That's close to Spector, who has a job and, for argument's sake, is a good family man.' In fact, Bundy was actually married, another similarity to Spector.

Jamie could appreciate that Spector was an extremely complex character. 'I truly believe he does love his children, weirdly,' he continued. 'I never doubted that he was a good father, which makes it all so harrowing. I also think he's a relatively good husband. I don't think he's ever cheated on his wife. I'm not saying, "Cut the guy a break. He's misunderstood." But I think there are core qualities he adheres to in terms of family.'

Even Jamie found some of the scenes disturbing, however. 'Within five minutes he goes from washing his daughter's hair to stalking and planning the next attack. That's what makes the heinous bits so shocking: he's a husband and he's a father. Not only that, he's a good father. I don't want to play a serial killer for the rest of my life but this will change perceptions of who I am.' That was certainly true. Quite apart from anything else, Jamie's acting abilities made it clear once and for all that he was not getting cast just because of the way he looked.

There was a good deal of fascination with Gillian Anderson, as well, who was compelling in her role as policewoman Stella, who realizes what is happening long before her colleagues do. Anderson, who first found fame in *The X Files* in 1993, playing Agent Scully, was now playing a glacial blonde whose cool appearance concealed a complicated personality. She too attracted enormous praise for her role, which she said she was initially drawn to because of the quality of the writing.

'[Like] most jobs that come my way, it came first in the form of a script,' Gillian told *npr.org*. 'And there's something about [creator] Alan Cubitt's writing that kind of gets under your skin. So from the moment I turned the first page, I couldn't put it down for his writing. But I was also very intrigued by this character of Gibson and didn't feel like I'd really read a character like her before, encountered a character quite like her before. And she continues to remain an enigma for me.'

Of course, there had been another very famous fictional lady detective –DCI Jane Tennison in *Prime Suspect*, who was played by Helen Mirren – and Gillian was happy to acknowledge the debt. 'I'm a huge fan of Helen Mirren, that goes without saying,' she continued. 'I think it was always something that I held in the back of my mind as something to aim for. And [*The Fall*] could have gone a few ways in the way that it was shot, and it certainly could have been shot differently and felt more Americanized. And I felt very strongly, because of *Prime Suspect*, that it [should have] a grittiness to it. It . . . has a European flavour and it comes off the page.' Indeed, it had something of the Nordic thrillers that were becoming so popular at the time.

Unlike Jamie, Gillian wasn't actually a native of Belfast, but she too felt that something of the city's haunting melancholy made a contribution to the series. 'It definitely does,' she told *Digital Spy*. 'I hope what it ends up doing is unveiling Belfast in a new way. We properly show the city – it's not just interiors the whole time. It gives a really positive spin on the beauty and complexity of the city itself, rather than just the history and the politics of it. By filming there as opposed to filming in London, you're not seeing the same locations you're used to seeing all the time if you're watching British series. But also, there's a tension – just the fact that it's in Belfast, there's a tension. It's just there – it breathes in the city and I think it comes across on-screen.'

Gillian saw great parallels between her own character and that of Paul Spector, in that both characters are hunters. 'Oh yes,' she said. 'What I find intriguing is that there aren't that many degrees difference between all of us and somebody who is able to do something like Spector – and I find that fascinating. That becomes quite evident in the way this is written and shot, with the parallel storylines. I think she absolutely knows where he comes from, and it's not from "over there" – it's from somewhere closer.'

That wasn't all. Both characters were so glacial as to be utterly indifferent to normal human emotion, Stella quite as much as Paul. She becomes fascinated by a tribe of Chinese women who rule the roost in their neck of the woods, do not marry and invite the men for one-off 'sweet nights' in which they meet to have sex but the men are expected to leave in the morning with no further relationship expected. 'Who', one character asks the sexually voracious Stella, 'would be stupid enough to get into bed with a man she had only just met?'

The Fall began its first series on 13 May 2013 on BBC Two, followed shortly afterwards in the US on Netflix, with the episode 'Dark Descent', in which the viewer sees Stella Gibson fly from London to Belfast to investigate a murder, which she quickly realizes is probably not the killer's first. A serial killer is on the loose. At the same time Paul is pictured at work as a bereavement counsellor, drawing wildly inappropriate pictures of a sobbing mother who has lost a child, and living an utterly ordinary life with his wife and two children, until he breaks into the house of a solicitor and leaves items of underclothing on her bed. Terrified, the woman calls the police, who investigate and find nothing, unwisely assuming there is nothing wrong as she had been drinking and got a little confused. The woman herself asks them to leave, but when she wakes up she sees an orange peel left by Paul, who had eaten it in her kitchen. We know tragedy will strike and it does.

Critics and viewers loved it from the start. 'Why is it so compelling?' asked David Thomson in the *New Republic*. 'I think it's because this show is breaking new ground; Gillian Anderson said as much in a promotional interview. It's what made her want to do it. There is a secret similarity between Stella and Paul Spector, the killer. It begins in habits: they are both athletic – he runs; she swims. They are loners and intellectuals; their belief in intelligence is what makes them unreachable and unknowable. They both cherish the ritual of preparation. When we first see Stella, getting ready to go to Belfast, she removes a covering of nocturnal face cleanser. It's like the way Paul works behind a mask.'

Willa Paskin, writing in *Salon*, agreed. 'The Fall, a five-episode crime series from the BBC that debuted on Netflix last week, is a kind of compendium of contemporary TV cool: tortured serial killer, complex female lead, specific and loaded setting, a slow pace that prioritizes psychology and character over crime solving,' she wrote. '(Like so much else, its leading influences are the original *Prime Suspect* and the original *The Killing*.) It takes all these tropes and tosses them into a creepy, classy, artful series that is so totally of the now it hardly matters that it's not quite as good as it could be. It looks and feels like the right thing, the kale salad of crime shows. I ate it all up.'

'It's a fine show, relying on slow-building tension rather than the gory shock value of series like *The Following*, and the five-episode arc now on Netflix is worth a look if you haven't had your fill of cat-and-mouse dynamics. If, on the other hand, you're watching more than two serial-killer series already and feel the need for more, you may want to ask yourself what this says about you,' said a somewhat tongue-in-cheek Neil Genzlinger in the *New York Times*. 'Anyway, Ms Anderson is Stella Gibson, a police investigator who is brought in to jump-start a stalled murder case in Belfast, Northern Ireland . . .

'While the investigation is gearing up, we are also given glimpses of the killer, Paul Spector (Jamie Dornan), a grief counselor with a seemingly idyllic life – pleasant wife, two cute young children – but an exceedingly dark side. He doesn't just kill; he carefully studies and stalks his intended victims, collects mementos of them and arranges their bodies in poses. Each side in this law-versus-lawbreaker game is meticulous.'

'*The Fall* has certainly earned its plaudits. At times captivating, it was rarely less than atmospheric, intense and dark. It was generally well-acted, and, refreshingly, there was a certain plausibility to the nature of and motives behind the killings,' wrote David Hynes in *What Culture*.

'A fantastically creepy thriller shaped by the heroine's feminism and unapologetic sexuality,' was Caryn James' verdict on *James on Screens*. 'Anderson's delivery is sharp as her jaw in a series smarter and richer than most.'

Jose Solis' take on it in *PopMatters* was also enthusiastic. '*The Fall*'s intention of revealing the dangerous connection between sex and death isn't only audacious, but also endlessly seductive,' was how he put it. It was official: the show was a massive hit – and Jamie had proved conclusively that he could act.

The series continued with wonderfully deft touches. Paul's young daughter, to whom he is very close, has a series of terrible nightmares, prompted, perhaps, by sensing without understanding it what a monster her father really is. She also wears a necklace he gave her even at night, prompting her grandmother to point out that it might strangle her (Paul's method of dispatching his victims). 'It's not a dream,' she tells her mother, adding that she has seen a lady with no clothes on in the space above her bed (where her father keeps his macabre notebook). And so it went on.

In the last episode (spoiler alert) Paul's back story begins to emerge. He spent his childhood in care homes; he has no friends or family of his own. It is left to his wife, to whom he has made up the lie that he has been having an affair, to point out that she was never able to get to know him in the way most people get to know others, namely through their relationships with their nearest and dearest. 'It scares me,' she says.

'Don't be scared,' her serial killer husband replies.

In the meantime he and Stella finally set eyes on each other in the flesh: there is not only obvious mutual attraction but also a hint of recognition. They are the good and evil sides of the same coin. The game of cat and mouse they have been playing throughout the series becomes very personal. One of the victims' fathers was allowed to broadcast a television appeal for his daughter's murderer to come forward to promise that if he stops his terrible actions and repents of his past crimes, then he will have 'a one-on-one conversation with me'. However, the poor man collapses and is unable to go on, leaving Stella to read his original words, watched on television by Paul. Only when she reads out the lines about the conversation, he presumes this one-to-one conversation will be with her.

When the two of them do finally speak, it is Paul who points out the similarities between them. Both are driven and seek power and control he tells her. But while she is bound by convention, he is 'free'.

'How are you free?' demands Stella, telling him that he is weak, impotent, a 'slave to your desires'. 'You think you're some kind of artist but you're not.' The two taunt and goad one another. It's almost like flirting in reverse.

All of this is set against a background that is very Belfast. In a secondary storyline, instances of police corruption arise – in fact, it is never entirely clear quite how far that corruption goes up the hierarchy – and a near riot breaks out when a murder and a botched murder take place in one of the more dangerous part of the city – a sign that the Troubles are not, alas, over.

The series ended somewhat ambiguously, with Paul and his family heading off to find a new life. How could it not? By now the BBC had realized it had a massive hit on its hands and had commissioned a second series before the first one had come to an end. Consequently they had to let Paul get away – had he been caught, there'd be no more drama to wring out of it. As it was, everything was up in the air.

'From a fine beginning to an absolutely stonking end,' wrote Gerard O'Donovan in the *Daily Telegraph*. 'Even in the wake of last week's sofa-munchingly scary cliffhanger, I half-expected the concluding episode of BBC Two's *The Fall* would be a terrifying yet conventional cop-drama race to the finish, leaving the killer in jail, the kids tucked up in bed and the world a safe and comfy place again. I couldn't have been more wrong. Instead we got a gripping, slow-burning, brilliantly constructed tease, with ice-cold supercop Stella Gibson (Gillian Anderson) inching ever closer to ever-madder serial killer Paul Spector (Jamie Dornan) – only to have him walk away at the end like Hannibal Lecter, free to strike terror into us all over again.'

It had been a tour de force from everyone involved and had produced (with very good timing, as it happens) a major new star. As Jamie began to realize he was now a fully fledged star, he began to ponder on his own technique, almost shyly at first, as if he couldn't quite realize what a leap he'd made. 'I wasn't aware of it at first, but the way I used my hands became a way for me to play Spector's awareness,' he told *Interview* magazine. 'You see the difference in how he deals with his family, with his kids, and the way he approaches other things in his life.'

And how did he create such a monstrous character? 'A lot of that's done for me, on the page, in [*The Fall* creator Allan Cubitt's] mind,' he continued. 'The occupation he's given Spector, the family he's given Spector, and the life he's given Spector; I'm just trying to play that. What is creepy about that is the normality of it all. He's a grief counsellor, of all things. He has a wife and two kids that I think he loves. I think Allan would say that Spector's incapable of love and therefore doesn't love the kids. I would try to argue that slightly. I would say that he portrays a certain form of love, certainly to his daughter. In a way, I don't think Spector's that bad of a husband. He can be a bit despondent. And it's crazy saying that, when you see what he's getting up to, but I actually don't think that negates the good qualities that he has as a husband and a father. I think he shows good qualities, despite the fact that he hunts and kills innocent women. It is all quite sordid. But I want to show how regular these guys can be.'

That was, of course, part of what contributed to the creepiness of his portrayal. But Jamie even managed to find some positive quality within Paul. 'I would go as far as to say "like",' he said. 'I don't think I'll ever play a character that I don't have some fondness for, or who doesn't have some redeeming quality to me. I'm not sure I'll play anyone more heinous than Paul Spector in my life, but I might, and I will only do that if I find something within him that is sort of acceptable. For Spector, despite all the horrendous acts, there's something that I'm fond of in his character, and I think a lot of those characteristics in him I admire, he uses for quite odious purposes. I wish I had his attention to detail, and his efficiency. I think you've got to learn something from every character you play. You've got to take something away, as an actor, as a person.' He'd taken a huge amount: he'd run with it and made the part his own. But what next? A second series of *The Fall*, of course, but Jamie was now edging towards that enviable state that every actor dreams of: he was going to be able to start picking and choosing his roles from now on – rather than taking them just because the mortgage had to be paid.

Looking dapper at the *GQ* Awards, where Jamie picked up the Vertu Breakthrough Artist Award.

Producers hired Jamie not only for his acting talent and gorgeous looks, but because of his sizzling chemistry with co-star Dakota Johnson.

Fans were delighted to hear that Dornan would be playing Christian Grey after Charlie Hunman dramatically dropped out of the leading role.

Not one to rest on his laurels, Jamie has starred in various TV and film projects since signing up for *Fifty Shades of Grey*, including Channel 4's *New Worlds*.

Charming the British public on *The Graham Norton Show*.

Getting into character: Jamie channels the enigmatic Christian Grey on the set of *Fifty Shades of Grey*.

Life will never be the same again for the normal lad from Northern Ireland.

A natural in front of the camera, Jamie's modelling career prepared him well for future high-profile TV and film projects.

Mr Grey will see you now: Jamie smoulders as the bondage-obsessed billionaire.

10

A Star Is Born

J amie's life had changed completely, in a way that was totally new, even after *Once Upon a Time*. His ability to play a monster who was also a family man had catapulted him into the international spotlight in a way that actors dream of but few actually attain. And his timing couldn't have been better: *The Fall* aired in spring 2013, at exactly the moment the producers of *Fifty Shades of Grey* were debating who to cast in what would undoubtedly be the blockbuster of the year. They hadn't alighted on him yet, but Jamie had proved he could play a brooding man with a troubled past, giving the character a depth that set the screen alight. *The Fall* hadn't exactly been an audition for the hottest film role in years, but it certainly didn't hurt his chances.

His fellow actors were happy to talk about him, too, not least because they saw his status change when the series aired: it was happening right in front of their eyes. When the casting was first announced, it was Gillian who was the big star, and although she unquestionably maintained that status, she was privy to Jamie's massive breakthrough. And she, along with fellow cast members, wanted to make it very clear that in real life Jamie was nothing like the character he played. Indeed, no one had a bad word to say about him.

'He's just one of the loveliest young men and I'm really happy for him with his success and his family . . . he's a great guy,' she told the *Belfast Telegraph* as speculation about a second series began. 'Jamie is just the sweetest, nicest guy you could ever meet and no he hasn't changed at all. Of course he will be back if we are all back. You know if he says he is leaving us, I'll give him a good slap and change his mind!'

There was no chance of that happening. As Jamie himself has often pointed out, most scripts are complete dross and if you are presented with a good opportunity you seize it. This had been his breakthrough, and he was hardly going to let it slip away now. There comes a moment in the lives of most successful people when they shift up a gear and life changes, and this was Jamie's moment.

Bronagh Waugh, who played Paul's wife Sally Ann, was equally effusive, wishing to make it clear beyond a doubt that Jamie was not the character he was playing and that he was in fact a very nice, sociable man. As for the sex appeal: 'I get asked that all the time,' she told *IN!* magazine on the subject not only of playing a serial killer's wife but on making out with a former Calvin Klein model. 'He's just Jamie. When you're an actor and you work on the set all the time, it's just a work thing. The interest is weird. Our intimate scenes are the least intimate moments ever. For a start there are forty people in the room. I remember we did this one scene in the bath, and the water had to be still, no bubbles. I got in and lay down and I see Jamie's shoulders going like this (shakes) and I look down and there's my modesty cover floating down the bath, so when things like that happen, it's the most unromantic, unsexy thing ever.' Indeed, according to Bronagh, the association with Jamie was already helping her professionally. 'I went for an audition once and I think I was only called in because I'd worked with Jamie,' she continued. 'It's just a really weird thing and I'm like "Yes, but did you see the show? Did you like the show?".'

Over in Belfast, Jamie's father Jim had noticed the change too. Previously in the local community the status had been 'Jim Dorman's son Jamie is an actor'; now it was becoming 'Jamie Dornan's father Jim is an eminent doctor'. Not that Jim minded in the slightest: he was delighted by Jamie's success and thrilled that his son was doing so well. It couldn't have been easy watching him play his latest role, however. 'I watched [Jamie] in *The Fall* and thought he was great, but it was also a bit scary, seeing your son play a murderer,' he told the *Irish News*, adding that one viewer had remarked that at least 'he was a murderer who cleaned up after himself'. They were all thrilled, though. They had watched as Jamie strove to make it from those very early days when he was living in a hovel in London and trying to make it as a model. Now, after a very hard slog, he was turning into a real star. 'We as a family are justly very proud of Jamie – he's talented and grounded and a credit to his school (Methody), his amazing friends, his family and himself,' Jim went on.

There was more good news on the way, too. Marriage really suited Jamie, giving him the stability that every major star needs if they are to stand a chance of retaining any normality: it's essential to stay grounded or there's a danger you could crash and burn. That was unlikely to happen to such a self-deprecating man as Jamie, but other potentially huge stars of the future had gone that way in the past, so a solid relationship was all the more crucial.

Speculation was mounting that Jamie's wife Amelia was pregnant and in June 2013, his stepmother Samina gave the game away. As an obstetrician, she was ideally placed to give Amelia her first scan, and this she duly did at Belfast's 3fivetwo Healthcare clinic on Lisburn Road. 'Jim and I are delighted that our third grandchild is on the way,' she said to the *Belfast Telegraph*. 'The early wellbeing scanning was a beautiful and emotional experience for all present.' It was a nice change for Jamie, too. The world and his wife had been emphasizing that he and Paul Spector had absolutely nothing in common and in the pursuit of his role he'd had to go to a very dark place. What better to banish the memories of that than the news of the arrival of his first child?

Behind the scenes, his family was as close as ever. Jamie's sister Jessica was now a fashion designer based in Falmouth (somewhat appropriately, given that her brother started out as a model), while his sister Liesa was based in London and working for Disney. Liesa was, in fact, enjoying a high-flying career: after studying at Glasgow Caledonian University and the Chartered Institute of Marketing (ironic, given that Jamie had dropped out of his marketing degree), she had started working as a marketing manager for Ulster Weavers, before becoming UK Licensing Manager at Marvel Entertainment. She then moved to The Walt Disney Company, where she became first EMEA Toys Manager and then Franchise Manager – in other words, exactly the sort of career Jamie would have had if he had stuck with his studies instead of opting for modelling. Both sisters were as proud as their father about what Jamie was achieving, while adjusting to the fact that their brother was becoming a major star.

Meanwhile, despite the acting acclaim, Jamie continued to do some modelling; it may not have brought him the same job satisfaction as acting, but it certainly paid the bills. But was he enjoying his new status? Who wouldn't? He and Gillian gave a joint interview to *Red* magazine, including a larky photoshoot of the two of them dressed in evening wear and jumping about together, and the chemistry between them was obvious. They had shared almost no screen time together – just passing once in a corridor and a telephone call – but off-screen they clearly got on like a house on fire. Gillian still appeared the grande dame of the acting world to Jamie's ingénue, but both were clearly enjoying one another's company and feeding off the other's talent.

The interview read like a jolly chat between the two of them. 'You read so much shit,' Jamie confided about roles he had previously been offered, as it emerged that initially he had auditioned for a role as a police officer in the series, before it occurred to someone that he might be pretty good as the lead. His sensitivity to having started out as a model was still extremely evident, though.

'I don't know if I get sent more than other people, and some of that might be to do with the fact that I modelled, but very often I get pushed towards a similar type of role,' he continued. 'Usually it's the character that, two pages before the end, kisses a girl and that's that. It's so rare that a character this good would even be an option for me. I didn't think I'd have a chance in hell of playing Spector. I've never been on British television before, so for my first thing to be something as good as this . . .'

'Yeah, they made you jump through some hoops,' Gillian said. 'But I think it was pretty clear from the beginning that you were the man for the job. I just think it was a matter of convincing the powers that be. I've been in the same situation before, with people fighting my corner, but having to convince studios that you're the one – it takes some effort.' Gillian spoke from experience, having become famous as Scully when she was still a very young woman. But every actor, no matter how good, has to soak up a good deal of indifference and scepticism at the outset and she was no different. This was another reason the two of them sparked off each other so well: she had been through what Jamie was going through, but as a well-established actress herself, she didn't see him as competition. Instead, she wanted to help him and give him advice.

Of course Gillian had enjoyed herself too. *The Fall* had not just made a star out of Jamie: it was an excellent television show that had provided her with a great role. Gillian, who is now based in the UK, had been cast in some very high-profile shows before, not least *Great Expectations*, but she, along with everyone else, knew that this series stood out. 'I think Stella is probably one of my favourite characters I've played,' she said. 'I haven't figured out how to say this without it sounding bad, but I feel like Stella is closer to me than any-body I've played before. It's just I usually say that after I say I think she's really cool. I know! It doesn't come out so good. But I really like her as a woman, I like her more as a woman than me. I think there's something really cool about her.' Actually, she was spot on – that was what made Stella such a compelling character to watch. And as for the fact that Gil-lian related to her – well, the slight embarrassment might have stemmed from the fact that Stella is sexually voracious, but there was also the fact that she was in charge in a man's world, that she could take control, was competent and that slightly glacial quality hinted at fires that roared within. Stella was as compelling a character as Paul and for many of the same reasons – both clearly had something to hide.

Listening to the banter between the two actors during the *Red* interview was very instructive – they were clearly not just learning something from each other but supporting each other too. Both had discovered that when they left their nat-ural backgrounds and ended up somewhere else, they found opportunities they wouldn't have before. 'Modelling doesn't hold you back in LA at all,' said Jamie, harking back to a familiar theme. 'In LA, they don't think that because you leant against walls and looked depressed while someone took your photograph, it means you can't act. In the UK, there's a massive stigma attached to it. You couldn't possibly have had your photograph taken for a living and act.'

'It's so weird, because my experience is completely opposite,' said Gillian. 'When I first moved here, I was offered *Bleak House*, which was so different to anything I'd ever done before. Not in a million years would I have got a role like that in the States. There was a belief here that, even though I'd done Scully, I could do period drama, too. I wanted to say to them, "Why do you think I can do this?" '

'But Scully is a really fucking interesting character in a massive show, and you're really impressive in it,' said Jamie, who was clearly incapable of opening his mouth without being charming and complimentary. 'So that's nine years of constantly being impressive as an actress, whereas I've got nine years of leaning against walls – and it treated me very well, but it was almost to my detriment as an actor.'

'It's just going to take a couple of things like this and that will change,' Gillian assured him, and of course, she was right. Jamie's ongoing insecurity about his modelling past was not just a random thing: he really had had to put up with a lot of nonsense from people who didn't think you could move from one profession to another. Clearly he could still hardly believe those days were over and that the public's perception of him had totally changed.

Gillian had her own issues to contend with, though, and they were considerably more practical than the angst felt by her co-star. She'd had to commute between London, where she was now based, and Belfast, to shoot the series, but the fact that she was prepared to do so again bore testament to the quality of the script. 'It's all timing and scheduling and what I'm in the mood for,' she continued. 'For me, everything is about schedules. But with this, once I recognized I had fallen in love with it and was determined to make it work, there were ways to compromise. It's also about choosing things I don't feel like I've ever done before. I see actors who have done sixty films that are the same and I think, How do you even show up any more? If I sense I'm doing something I've done before, it drives me insane.' It was not a problem Jamie had had to deal with yet, but even so, the roles he had played to date were all so completely different that it boded well for the future.

Red were also keen to know how they'd got on when filming in situ: the answer was fine when they saw one another, but in actual fact that hadn't happened very often. It turned out that Jamie had not shown her around Belfast, mainly because she was rarely there during down time between shooting; she was either hunkering down in her hotel or returning to London to be with her family. She was, she admitted, something of a hermit. Jamie, on the other hand, had enjoyed being home. It was rare that he was able to mix business with pleasure, his professional life with time in his home town, but for once, this had been the case during filming.

'For me, it was a very different experience,' he said. 'My dad's there, some of my best friends in the world are there.

I had an apartment in the middle of town for three months. And I've never actually lived in Belfast because I grew up just outside, so I experienced the city on a different level, waking up and going to get coffee and read the papers on my day off. I'd never done that, so I just loved it. And it's nice to not have to repeat yourself, as well, in terms of your accent!' It was certainly a first for Jamie: in every role he had played to date he had had to conceal his Northern Irish accent, but in this case it was a positive bonus since Jamie was from the same place as the character he was playing.

It wouldn't be the case for long, though. As his date with destiny approached, Jamie would soon have to adopt a Seattle twang, as he was about to be cast as Christian Grey.

As mentioned earlier, he had returned just the once to *Once Upon a Time*, and whatever the truth about whether he'd wanted to leave the show, he couldn't have gone back now even if he'd wanted to, as he had too much on his plate.

Across the Atlantic in LA, the studio producers seemed a little taken aback by the turn of events, though they were nonetheless happy for their protégé. 'Last year, when he did "Welcome to Storybrooke" for us, it was fantastic to have him come back,' executive producer Edward Kitsis told *AccessHollywood.com*. 'He's a friend of ours, he's a friend of the show and unfortunately, this year, he goes right from the movie to *The Fall* . . .

'And it's funny . . . his part was always conceived as that seven-episode arc in the first season . . . with the hope we could bring him back here and there as we've done,' Adam

Horowtiz added. 'But . . . it's gratifying that everyone seems to have responded so well to his talent.'

How could he have come back, though? 'Ask us that after the finale,' Kitsis said. 'And then we'll tell you exactly what we wanted to do and you will be so bummed that we didn't get to do it, and then you will have the same look on your face that I do right now, which is sadness.'

'We miss him dearly,' Adam said.

'We're so happy for him,' Horowitz added.

'To be honest, we'd like to take credit for it, actually,' said Kitsis. 'We are his biggest fans.'

'We're very, very happy for him,' Horowitz said. 'Obviously . . . we'd love to have him if he ever wanted to come back, but he is quite busy right now, and rightfully so. He's very talented.'

He certainly was – although with that level of fame, Jamie was going to have to learn to cope with the huge amount of attention he would attract.

11

After the Fall

The year 2013 was going well for Jamie. The Keira connection was finally forgotten now that Jamie was married and Keira had tied the knot with her rock-star boyfriend James Righton, keyboard player for the Klaxons, and praise for *The Fall* was still being heaped upon him. Jamie himself was aware of how lucky he'd been: 'It was a risk and I was wholly aware of it,' he told *The Times*. 'I've never been the lead in anything, I've never done any work for British television, I've never been on British TV at all apart from an American show that was shown here, so I'm sure I wasn't on anyone's shortlist when they started thinking about casting. I would doubt I was even on a long-list, if I'm honest.'

It had achieved what he'd wanted it to, as well. After filming *The Fall*, but before the programme was broadcast, Jamie gave an interview to the *Sun*, in which the ongoing problem of being a model who'd moved into acting came up. 'Very few people who watch BBC dramas would know I was a model,' he'd said. 'If you do too much modelling I guess there's a stigma attached to it. I wanted to act from a young age, but other things got in the way, I guess. This isn't even close to anything I've done before. I'm keen for this to come out because I think it might change things a little bit.' In reality, it changed things completely. No one would ever be able to ask if he was just a pretty face again.

The series didn't just transform Jamie's life, it affected other cast member's lives too. The Irish actress Séainín Brennan, who like Jamie had enjoyed another career – in her case in European politics – played a secondary role in the series as the grieving mother that Paul counsels, thereby putting his life at risk of sectarian violence. '*The Fall* has been amazing in so many ways,' she told the *Daily Mirror*. 'I play Liz Tyler alongside Jamie Dornan as the serial killer Paul Spector and Gillian Anderson, who plays detective Stella Gibson. This has been my most challenging TV role to date, but I love the fact I'm hitting an area that is so difficult in real life. My character's lost her only child following a medical misdiagnosis, and the series starts three weeks after the child's death in that moment when the world goes quiet, the doorbell stops ringing and people stop calling. They give her space to gather up her life again but she is in desperate pain. So Liz seeks solace in Paul Spector but she has no idea he is a serial killer. Spector, in turn, begins to develop an unhealthy professional relationship with Liz in her most vulnerable state. In episode one Liz starts to take the audience on an emotional rollercoaster ride. She's deeply traumatized as she is going through the most difficult period of her life. The script was searingly real and it just caught my attention and I couldn't shake it. As an actor I need there to be enough truth in a script to get on board. And in this series, I pulled on experiences from two people I love who have been through this awful tragedy in real life.'

The writer, Allan Cubitt, who had previously worked on *Prime Suspect*, garnered enormous praise, too. He'd created this tremendously dark character for Jamie to portray, and it was something he was often asked about. 'To me he's not psychotic,' he told the *Daily Telegraph*. 'I think we're on a continuum with him. My fantasies are – thank God – not like his, but I understand what it's like to have a fantasy life. I'm a writer. And I'm also a man.' And was there a connection between his own fantasies and the programme? It was an uncomfortable question, which Allan bravely answered. 'That's probably quite an awkward question to answer,' he said. 'I'm glad to say I'm not given to violence, but I've been obsessed by people. The closest I would have come to insane behaviour is being in the grip of some romantic love that's gone badly wrong. My most jealous moments have probably been my most insane moments – when I've not been able to stop myself throwing things at windows or trying to kick down doors . . .'

The BBC did well out of it, too: BBC Two got its highest rated drama launch in five years with 15 per cent of the viewing total, or 3.5 million viewers. BBC head of drama Northern Ireland, Stephen Wright, was said to have been 'thrilled' by the news, and Ben Stephenson, controller of BBC drama, called it 'an outstandingly imagined piece of television'.

The only people who didn't seem to have done well out of it were, more surprisingly, members of the Northern Irish acting community. Drew McFarlane, Equity's national organizer for Northern Ireland and Scotland, wasn't pleased. 'We have a smashing series in *The Fall*, but look at the cast, most of the actors, even the Irish and Northern Irish ones, live in London,' he said. 'Actors who choose to live in Northern Ireland get walk-on roles. Local actors don't even have a fair crack of the whip because the initial casting and auditions are done in London before a production comes over to Northern Ireland. When that happens, all the locals get are cough and spit roles. I understand the argument that you need well-known faces in the leading roles, but an entire cast? Local actors need an opportunity to work in good television drama instead of just working three months of the year at the Lyric theatre. There has been an exodus of actors from Northern Ireland because they can't afford to live and work there. A complete exodus would have a knock-on effect on all cultural aspects of Northern Ireland. You'd think a public broadcaster funded by licence payers would do something.'

It was a rare dissenting note, though there were others: some commentators expressed disquiet at the violence, the very explicit scenes in which the victims met their end. And there was criticism, too, of the fact that Jamie was so good looking, and in many ways appealing in the role, that you almost overlooked the fact that his character was a violent and ruthless killer. Certainly, the makers of the series had gone as far as they could do with the violence and some felt they had overstepped the line.

Ben Stephenson, though, was increasingly pleased with every week that went by, and when the time came to announce the second series, he could barely contain himself: 'The Fall has proved a critical and ratings hit for BBC Two and a reminder of the resurgence of drama on the channel,' he said. 'With more of Allan Cubitt's thrilling plot revelations yet to unfold through the captivating performances of Gillian and Jamie, a second series is a must.

'Obviously we can't give too much away as the first series builds to a gripping cliffhanger but what we can say is it will be as surprising and intense as the first.'

Allan himself was equally delighted. 'The BBC has been an incredibly supportive partner in this project, and working with BBC NI and the Artists Studio has been the best experience of my career to date,' he said. 'I always envisioned *The Fall* as a returning series and wish to congratulate both Gillian Anderson and Jamie Dornan, who have played their parts to perfection.'

Allan also revealed that the inspiration behind Paul Spector was not Ted Bundy after all, but a depraved killer called Dennis Rader, who murdered ten people in Wichita, Kansas, and managed to avoid justice for the best part of forty years. 'Yes, Spector is Rader, to an extent,' he told *The Sunday*

Times. 'I was reading a book [*Bind, Torture, Kill: The Inside Story of BTK, the Serial Killer Next Door*] written by journalists who covered the Rader case in Wichita. Rader was a killer who bound, tortured and then killed, like Spector.

I liked the idea that both were living in medium-sized towns – about 500,000 – where you might have thought it would be easier to catch a serial murderer. I also wanted Spector to be normal. I liked his and Rader's normality. He was married with two children, like Rader, and held a reasonably responsible job.'

The real-life Rader killed between 1974 and 1991, almost entirely through suffocation or strangulation, and was caught after he sent a letter to the police. He was sentenced to ten life sentences (which he is still serving) with no prospect of parole. Like Spector, he too was an unlikely suspect: married with two children, he was a board president of the Christ Lutheran Church, was helpful to his neighbours and worked for a security company, installing alarms for people who were terrified by stories of a killer in their midst.

'What intrigues me about some serial killers is that they often have an arrogance that they can get away with what they do,' said Allan. 'They also have grandiose ideas. Those who are not psychotic, like Spector and Rader, know the difference between right and wrong at one level. One of the things that was fascinating about the book was that it opened with his perspective on his first attack. And I began to form an idea – it's quite a simple idea – that you identify who the killer is from the beginning, which is what we do . . . so it's not a whodunnit at all. There's no need for false suspects – you know who the killer is. The interest was in looking at how he did what he did, and the way he manipulated his victims, his family and the police.'

Accolades continued to pour in for Jamie. *The Sunday Times* asked him about the consequences of being recognized: 'I'm slightly worried,' Jamie acknowledged. 'Look, I don't get recognized a lot anyway, but I'm slightly anxious about how people will approach me – because, if you see someone being creepy on TV, you automatically assume that they're a creepy guy.'

He certainly hadn't lost his sense of humour, though. Now newly married to Amelia, the two watched the programme together, something you'd expect a new wife to find a little difficult. 'My wife hadn't seen the third episode, so we watched it the other night,' Jamie revealed. 'She was a little bit wary of me for about half an hour after it finished. I had to win back her trust. It's interesting. I guess I didn't quite realize I was capable of coming across as so dark. Everyone in the process of casting me must always have seen that darkness in me. Yet I'm not sure I even saw it myself. Basically, it must have been inside me, which is kind of worrying. In truth, I struggle [with watching it] a bit – we didn't film it in any sequential order. When you see it all put together, and the proximity of what he's doing at home with his kids and what he's doing at night, what he gets off on – I do struggle. I understand why people find that tough to watch.'

Despite his success, it seemed that Jamie was still fretting about modelling. 'I'd say that is something I will constantly battle with,' he said. 'It's okay for actors to become models and do campaigns, but if a model becomes an actor, it's instantly, "What's he trying? What a loser. There's no way he can act." But look, if I saw an interview with me and it said "model turned actor", I'd go, "Oh, God, who the f*** is this guy? Why does he think he can act?"'

He'd proved he could, though. 'I guess it's affirmation,' said Jamie, who clearly couldn't bear to admit that he had done a brilliant job. 'There will be so many people, no matter what I do, who won't accept me as an actor because I did a load of modelling. So there are going to be people – God, I know some of those people – who will always go, "That guy is a model who is trying to act." But it's a start. They can't take it away. I've done it and it exists, so I should be . . . I am proud of the show – really proud of it. I won't go as far as to say that I'm proud of myself.'

Jamie was clearly increasingly conflicted: on the one hand modelling had earned him a lot of money and provided him with a launch pad to greater stardom, but on the other hand he felt it was holding him back. There was also an issue that if he criticized the fashion industry, he could be biting the hand that fed him. There was no denying the fact that every part he played appeared to require him getting his top off pretty early on, and inevitably this drew comparisons with his previous career.

Jamie is in fact an enormously relaxed and agreeable per- sonality and he dealt with the issue easily and equably whenever it came up, which it did all the time. 'Mate, it doesn't get me excited, the idea of it,' he told *The Sunday Times*, carefully treading a fine line by saying that he'd moved beyond it without appearing to dump on the people who had used his services in the past, and who occasionally still did. 'I respect the industry massively, and I think it's cool. It's not like I don't look back on the stuff I did with a bit of pride. The reality is, you've got a mortgage, and actually it really helped. But I always, always knew I wanted out. I potentially did too much of it – it's detrimental. Do enough big, high-profile stuff, and it's not just, "He got his photograph taken." You become part of a brand. With Calvin Klein, that was me. So there's a danger that it's in too many people's psyches. I think I'm going to be constantly battling that label.' Certainly, he was having to deal with the kind of obsession over his appearance that is more usually the preserve of women. Headline writers had a field day, and strap lines such as 'If looks could kill' and 'It's fall happening for Jamie' didn't let anyone forget what Jamie had done earlier in his career.

This period seemed to be somewhat angst-ridden for Jamie. Not only was he fretting about his modelling, he was worried about what led to him being cast in *The Fall*. He had originally read for the role of a police officer and seemed concerned about the fact that he appeared to be more suited to the role of a maniac. 'Then the fear sets in,' he explained. 'Do I take offence that whatever I did in the room trying to play a detective, they saw the serial killer in me? Is that a compliment? Then there was the proper fear – I'm going to get fired at the table read, and they'll realize they've got it completely wrong.' It betrayed a great deal of insecurity, which was perhaps understandable in someone who was getting used to being a big name in the acting industry. It was as if Jamie's acting career had been rolling along in the slow lane and then quite suddenly accelerated to the speed of a plane taking off. It took some getting used to, both his own changing status and the reaction he was getting from his peers.

From Calvin Klein model to serial killer was quite a leap, and he couldn't help reassuring people that he was nothing like the character he played. The relaxed easy-going Jamie, who had a wonderful sense of humour in private and was happier than ever in the role of family man, couldn't help but be alarmed that people might actually equate him with a monster. He also didn't want to be typecast. 'In the meantime, I'd like to do something vastly different,' he said. 'Or, at least, I'd like to play someone who doesn't murder people. If I can, I'd like to do something light. By nature, I'm quite a light-hearted person. I like to have fun, I like to laugh. So in a perfect world, I'd like to do something funny.' In actual fact, of course, he was about to make headlines by signing up to play another damaged character, albeit one who didn't want to commit murder in his Red Room of Pain.

His fellow actors seemed to be equally keen to dispel the notion that Jamie was anything like the monster he played. 'Jamie is hand on heart one of the most down-to-earth, genuine people I have ever met in my life,' said Séainín Brennan to the *Mirror*. 'He is so nice and such a generous actor. They are the type of actors you want to work with. I do think the bigger the star the more generous they are as Philip Glenister was the same when I worked with him in *Hidden*.' She was keen to make it clear that her interest in him was strictly professional, though. 'And yes, Jamie is a lovely looking man, but he's a great actor and I have a lovely boyfriend who's a banker,' she continued.

By this time it had been confirmed that *The Fall* was coming back for a second series, though the actors weren't certain what form it would take. It was pretty much a given that Jamie and Gillian would be back, but as for everyone else? It was up in the air. Séainín spoke for the rest of the cast when she mentioned the uncertainty. 'Nobody knows yet who is going to be in it,' she went on. 'But from the minute I read the script for the first series I knew it was going to be phenomenal. It was a real page-turner and then we had a dream cast, too, and I think that is a big battle with any artistic project. The thing about it was that it is set in Northern Ireland but it's not about the Troubles, it's about something totally different. And it's now being seen all over the world, which is a brilliant success. You hope season two will have the same people in it, but I just want to see it regardless. I can only cross my fingers and hope I will be there, but even if I'm not, I'll still watch it.'

More acclaim followed when *The Fall* was nominated for Best Drama at the National Television Awards. Gillian was in the running for the new category of Best Detective, and the *Irish Mirror* awarded Jamie Newcomer of the Year.

As interest in him showed no sign of abating, Jamie was

asked how he went about his trade. In *The Fall*, there had been much comment about how he managed to express himself through using his hands, and he was asked by *Interview* magazine what the physicality of acting meant to him. 'It's a hard thing to define, "a physical actor",' he replied. 'Every role is physical to a certain extent, but as a viewer, I don't respond well to actors doing more than they need to tell a story. I get really thrown by that, and pissed off. Now and again an actor will blow my mind by doing something really unexpected, like Mickey Rourke or Christopher Walken – you have absolutely no idea what they're going to do, which is really thrilling to watch. And then there are actors who think they have the same quality as Mickey Rourke or Christopher Walken, and they just look really busy. They're doing lots of things, but they could just stand there and say the lines, and it would tell the story in a far more pleasing way for me personally.'

This was especially important when playing psychologically complicated characters and Jamie was already thinking about how he would apply this in the second series of *The Fall*. 'I find myself approaching it in a slightly less-is-more way,' he said. 'And once you get into something, once you've got those first couple of weeks out of the way, really mad or gallant things start to happen. With the second season of *The Fall* there is going to be more to him than I planned for. It's been over two years – I haven't stayed in his mind for the entire two years, don't worry – but when I'm in it, I do feel very comfortable in his skin, and that can only lead to rare things happening.'

Jamie had become one of a small group of actors who successfully work both in television and film. How did he reconcile the two? There were many people, after all, who felt that different styles of acting were required for each medium, and there are many television stars who come across well and are popular on the small screen, but who never achieve success in the cinema. How did he feel about that? 'I approach it all as the same thing,' Jamie told *Interview*. 'I've just finished watching *True Detective*, but I didn't watch it thinking that Matthew McConaughey and Woody Harrelson were acting for the small screen. I just thought they were fucking brilliant and giving epic performances. I think sometimes actors are drawn to good television because you have more time to sell it, you have more time to shape a character and to tell a story, and that's really appealing.'

And so it went on, every appearance he made was picked up on, every word analysed. Jamie was coping well, but even he must have been surprised at what trivia was attached to his name. When people start to become famous, their every utterance gets picked up on, and Jamie was no exception to that rule. *The Sunday Times* ran a men's fashion feature called 'I can't leave home without . . .' 'Sunspel does the best boxer shorts – I live in them. In fact, I only recently discovered it does clothing, too,' said Jamie, seguing somewhat effortlessly back into modelling mode. He was asked what his ideal job would be: 'If I could open a shop it would be part old-world toy shop, like the Cheshire Cat in Hillsborough, Northern Ireland, and part practical joke shop,' he told *The Times*. 'They were my favourite shops when I was a kid and everyone needs at least one water-squirting flower.'

Meanwhile, his acting career continued to develop. In July 2013, it was announced that Jamie would be taking part in a new drama called *New Worlds*. It was to be an historical drama, set in the Restoration era: '*New Worlds* is a compelling four-part drama capturing the political struggles of the period following the English Civil War both at home and overseas,' said Channel 4's Head of Drama, Piers Wenger. 'It has attracted a diverse and glittering cast and we're greatly looking forward to seeing their work brought to the screen.'

He was becoming a wealthy man, too, with properties in Notting Hill and the Cotswolds. He was reminded of the interview he'd given years earlier about Keira and how he couldn't match up to her at the time. Jamie, now a bona fide A-lister himself, appeared rather taken aback by his younger self. 'Did I really say that?' he asked, and indeed, it had been an uncharacteristic lapse of manners from someone who was widely talked of as being a really nice bloke. Jamie wasn't worried about that now, though. After all, he was set to conquer new worlds . . .

12

New Worlds

amie continued to veer back and forth between film and television; he was certainly proving himself to be versatile. From modelling to a fairy-tale hunter, followed by a serial killer and, it would later be announced, a romantic hero with an unfortunate proclivity towards S&M in *Fifty Shades*, he was now about to prove himself adept at period drama, too. He'd had a taste of that in *Marie Antoinette*, but it had been a small role in an unusual and not terribly authentic historical treatment. He was now set to start work on the Channel 4 period drama *New Worlds*.

Set in the 1680s, it was a sequel to a previous drama, *The Devil's Whore*, which had screened in 2008, and was set on both sides of the Atlantic. Although his involvement was announced before he got the part of Christian Grey, the series screened sometime afterwards, in the spring of 2014. Whether this was a good or bad thing depends on your point of view, because while Jamie's participation increased the show's profile, the series wasn't ultimately considered a success. Quite the opposite, in fact. For the first time, Jamie had to cope with the burden of expectation – having defied the critics who thought his modelling past meant he couldn't be a good actor, he now had to face people trying to knock him because he was successful. Jamie's life had changed fundamentally in a very short space of time, and there were plenty of envious rivals out there ready to snipe at him.

In *New Worlds*, Jamie played Abe Goffe, a 'young, idealistic renegade determined to end the monarchy's tyrannical rule'. In the words of the man himself, Abe is 'very determined in his fight to make England a true republic and end the tyrannical rule of the Stuarts throne', he told Channel 4. 'It is a similar fight to that taken up by his father William Goffe, who was a real historical figure and one whom Abe idolizes. He is trying to uphold the mantel of his father's campaign and muster support among others. He is headstrong, too much so at times, and is often quick to use his fists, but he learns during the course of the drama that there are better paths of action.' The series was directed by Charles Martin and written by Martine Brant and Peter Flannery, all of whom were well-respected names in television.

In essence the show had four main characters: Abe, Ned (Joe Dempsie from *Game of Thrones* and *Skins*), Beth (Freya Mavor, who also made her name in *Skins*) and Hope (Alice Englert). They were a very attractive young cast, but as is sometimes the way with these things, their good looks worked against them on the grounds that it made the series appear too lightweight. On the English side of the Atlantic, the monarchy has been restored: Charles II is on the throne and would appear to be running a regime of terror (hardly surprising, perhaps, given that his own father lost his head). This reaches as far as the States, where the New World is beginning to want to cast off the shackles of Imperialism and strike out on its own. However, they also had to take on what were then called American Indians, fighting them for land and generally oppressing them in much the same way they were oppressed by the British state.

There was, perhaps, a faint echo of the Hunter in Abe's character, since he was an outlaw. In the first episode, viewers saw the Countess of Seacourt, Angelica Fanshawe, attempting to keep her Catholic husband John Francis and her daughter Beth safe from a tyrannical world. Meanwhile, across the pond, struggles have begun. In the second episode John Hawkins sends his son Ned from Massachusetts to England to get away from the King's agents. Ned asks John to give Hope a letter, but instead he gets rid of it and insists that Hope marry Henry Cresswell, a widower, as it is improper for her to be a woman on her own. They live in a Puritan community and it is not the done thing.

Back in England, Abe and Beth have fallen in love and are both behaving like outlaws in Wightham Woods. Greedy landowner George Hardwick is, to all intents and purposes, treating his workforce like slaves, and so Abe and Beth blow up his clay pits. Meanwhile, in the background, Judge Jeffreys is gathering information to be used against Angelica and John. Abe then attempts to assassinate Charles II; when he fails, Angelica and Beth help him, for which they receive the death penalty. However Angelica manages to get this reduced to Beth's exile to the new world, which is where she goes.

It does not, however, go according to plan. In episode three, Beth is shipwrecked off the coast of Massachusetts before being rescued by the Wawanaki tribe of American Indians. Now back in Boston, Ned is upset that Hope is married to Henry, who just happens to be building a settlement on Wawanaki land, while Abe links up with Colonel Algernon Sidney and tries to assassinate Charles II once more. He fails again and the two are arrested. Ned meanwhile threatens Henry.

In the final episode Ned tells Hope that he wants to be with her but they must keep the fugitive Beth hidden away. Abe breaks out of prison, renounces violence and decides to spread Colonel Sidney's ideas instead. Wicked old Charles II finally dies and, on hearing the news, Beth decides to return to England, where she is reunited with Abe. Ned and Hope become revolutionaries. The end.

Everyone involved was keen to talk about their characters. 'To be honest, one of the things that really drew me to the script initially was the fact that Ned as a character, throughout the course of the series, goes on the longest journey, for lack of a less drama-school term,' Joe told *redcarpetnewstv. com*. 'He becomes the moral compass of the piece. You saw in episode one there the seeds of doubt starting to be planted in his mind.'

Freya was also very keen on her role. 'We meet her [Beth]

on her twenty-first birthday, when she's about to become a woman,' she told the *Daily Mail*. 'Until that point she has been living a sheltered life, blissfully unaware of the horrors that are going on in England – but that's about to change.' She then gets abducted: 'She puts up a fight, of course, but the truth is that there's an instant attraction between them,' Freya continued. 'She's going to fall in love with him [Abe] but she's also going to experience a total political awakening.'

As for Alice – 'For me Hope Russell is the original young American,' she told Channel 4. 'Her world is divided by what is right and wrong, good and bad, a simplicity that has always been prevalent in the American dream and American culture. Young, idealistic, fierce and vengeful, she lives on the fringes of the new world. But as her story progresses, Hope realizes the old world is inexplicably intertwined with the new and that she must navigate the complexity of being a child of a country where too much blood has been shed on both sides to ever be the dream it aspires to be.'

It was a young, inspired and committed cast who all cared a great deal about their roles. It was pretty harmless fare, and would probably have been little commented upon were it not for the fact that in the interval between casting and broadcasting, Jamie had turned into an A-list star. By this time he could hardly leave the house without making headlines, and the interest in his forthcoming role in *Fifty Shades* was so intense that it was bound to have an impact on the commentary on *New Worlds*.

Even without *Fifty Shades of Grey*, Jamie had attracted

such widespread attention and praise for *The Fall* that there would still have been interest in his next project. So how did his part compare with the role of Paul Spector? Given that one was a brutal serial killer and the other an idealist fighting for a more humane society, the similarities weren't immediately obvious, but Jamie was happy to find something to say nonetheless.

'Of course there are no comparisons between the two of them but I like playing characters who are passionate about something,' he told Channel 4. 'It is appealing as an actor to play characters who take care, precision and put commitment into something they are passionate about. In the case of Paul Spector that is the act of hunting and killing and covering up his crime, and obviously it is a very different motivation with Abe but he is equally a focused man with what he sees as a very clear objective. It is exciting to play such strong characters.'

Jamie did his homework, too. This was a real historical period, after all, and many of the characters, not least the wicked King Charles, were real people. Jamie was keen to read up on the period and discover what would have motivated a man like Abe, and the kind of struggles he would have had to endure. The other cast members were doing the same. 'A couple of books were suggested to us; there was one book *Cavalier* by Lucy Worsley that I know Freya and I both read and which was recommended to us by Martine Brant,' he said. 'It became a joke competition between Freya and I to finish it, my copy was more subtly on my iPad but Freya constantly lugged her copy around everywhere with her as I teased and tested her knowledge! Because I went to school in Belfast the English Civil War wasn't high on the curriculum, so to some extent I had to learn from scratch.' The Northern Irish accent was banished again, as Jamie turned himself into a convincing Englishman – more proof, if any were needed, of his acting abilities.

Jamie's star was so much in the ascendant that he could have had the pick of any parts he wanted, so what drew him to this role? 'Essentially it was the script first, then the character that I felt I could play, felt intrigued by and would hopefully interest an audience, and then I hoped I would get on with the director and everyone else involved,' he told Channel 4. 'On all these counts I have been so lucky with *New Worlds*. Peter Flannery and Martine Brant have worked so well together on this drama and I don't think Peter has ever written a bad script, so you know you are getting the best.' Jamie was not just speaking as an actor but as a viewer, he went on to confess. In many ways he was living through a golden era of television, and he was very aware of the opportunities. 'I really enjoy good TV drama, I was gripped by *Broadchurch* and thought *Southcliffe*, which Joe [Dempsie] is in, was brilliant, and I am a big *Sopranos*, *Curb Your Enthusiasm* and *Arrested Development* fan, and more recently I've been watching *Homeland*,' he said. 'We are so spoilt for choice with good television these days.' He was right there.

And Jamie's enthusiasm went into putting a lot of thought into his characters, giving them their own back story and justifying the way he portrayed them to the wider world. Inevitably, the comparisons to *The Fall* and his character continued, and Jamie was able to see the link. In fact, he was beginning to see links with a lot of the characters he played. 'I think he's broken, too,' he said of Abe in *Interview* magazine. 'I see broken people as those who have been through hardship – whether it's really ugly hardship like abandonment, abuse, something definitively life altering, like Christian Grey.'

Jamie had a heavy workload lined up post *New Worlds*: not just *Fifty Shades*, but the second series of *The Fall*, about which there was mounting expectation. 'Maybe in the second series of *The Fall* we will find out why Spector is the way he is – so I don't want to say too much about that,' he continued. 'But there are reasons for these people being the way they are, and that's what drives them. I think for Abe, he felt an injustice had been done to him. He was studying medicine when he was younger and couldn't continue because his father was one of the guys who signed the death warrant of Charles I. So that spurred him on.'

Unlike Paul Spector, however, Abe was able to develop and grow into a better person, something the viewers witnessed as the series progressed. Jamie had thought about that, too, it seems: 'Well, the thing about Abe was there's a lot of talk, and he is one of those people who talks with his fists,' he told *Interview*. 'As time goes on, over the four episodes, he has a massive change where he actually realizes that maybe words are the way forward. But you meet these guys in any time period who are very headstrong. I have mates like that who are just fucking aggressive. They move a certain way, especially around other people, around new people. They bristle up a little bit. And I tried to draw on some of that for Abe. He isn't comfortable with company outside of his select few.'

What could go wrong? The series appeared to have everything going for it: a handsome young cast, all of whom were thoughtful, considered and clearly passionate about the project they were embarking upon and who were all at the peak of their abilities. British television was good at historical dramas and there was no reason to think this series wouldn't work. There was character development, complex political issues that resonated with the present day (filming took place at the same time as another upsurge in Egypt, which was something the cast commented upon), professional writers with years of experience in television – in short every ingredient you could possibly have desired for success. But for some reason it didn't quite gel. Anyone hoping for a success along the line of *The Fall* – albeit with a vastly different subject matter – was not going to get their wish.

Sadly, the critics were not impressed. A great many elements were held up for criticism, including the fact that it didn't live up to its predecessor, *The Devil's Whore*, and – although no one said this overtly – a great deal more was expected from Jamie these days. Growing fame might have many advantages, but it also means increased levels of expectation and so a project that might have come in for mild criticism had it cast lesser-known actors became the focus of much sharper comment from people who associated Jamie entirely with success.

The critics were blunt in their summing up: 'Channel 4's new Tuesday night drama *New Worlds* was billed as a sequel to the 2008 drama *The Devil's Whore*, in which Andrea Riseborough and John Simm shone bright as a passionate 17th-century pair whose beliefs drew them right to the epicentre of the Civil War in England,' wrote Gerard O'Donovan in the *Daily Telegraph* in a review that was typical. 'Sadly, *New Worlds*, once again created by Peter Flannery and Martine Brant, and featuring another eye-catching cast of up-and-coming actors, displayed few of its qualities . . . There was nothing much any of these actors could do with a script and direction that clunked along lamely and rarely got into any kind of flow.'

Ellen E Jones, writing in the *Independent*, agreed. 'Despite their derring-do, this new cast of *Skins* graduates and ex-models didn't quite live up to *The Devil's Whore* originals, a group that memorably included Peter Capaldi, Dominic West, John Simm and Michael Fassbender,' she wrote. 'Riseborough, with her 17th-century beauty and timeless screen presence, was particularly missed. Idealists might be inspiring in the pages of history books, but they don't make for captivating TV characters. Let's hope this idealism will be compromised and motivations complicated in part two.'

David Stephenson in the *Sunday Express* wrote a very amusing review. 'The first twenty minutes was incomprehensible,' he said. 'On both sides of the Atlantic, it was kicking off. The problem was trying to establish what "it" was. In the "New World", the Indians were attacking the new settlers, which is where the phrase, "heads will roll", must originate. Meanwhile, back in Blighty, Charles II was on the throne, in vengeful mood, as Dornan and his merry band of Robin Hood-type thugs were busy poaching a deer (not cooking), before slicing open its throat in the grounds of a pleasant Oxfordshire stately home. It was property porn meets a six-part series on box hedging from Alan Titchmarsh.'

Hugo Rifkind in *The Times* was a little kinder. 'The *White Queen* last year was bad historical drama partly because it was a soap with nothing to say,' he wrote. 'Set two centuries later, in 1680, *New Worlds* is better partly because it knows exactly what's on its mind.'

The influential website *Den of Geek* was also kinder. 'We've not forgotten *The Devil's Whore*,' said villainous Judge Jeffreys in a much-needed exposition scene in the *New Worlds* opener,' it wrote. 'With any luck, neither will have the viewers because tonight's hour cut little slack for anyone dozing at the back . . . *New Worlds* clearly aspires to be more than just another swords-and-ripping-bodices historical romp, but presently its ambition is more appealing than either its story or characters. With the handsome stage set and many of the introductions out of the way now, though, there's every reason to expect more from Peter Flannery's unusual, politically charged drama in the coming weeks. Until then.'

As ratings continued to plummet, it was commented on that not even Jamie's presence could save it – a tribute to his star power, if not the actual show itself. Increasingly Jamie was seeing the downside of what it is to be a big name. He was criticized for his hairstyle (a 'mullet') and everything else anyone could think of. All in all it was quite a disappointment – albeit just a blip in a career that was going from strength to strength.

By now, Jamie had other things on his mind. Married life was going swimmingly and he was giving back to the community in which he'd grown up by becoming the patron of TinyLife, a charity for premature babies, of which his father was president. Then in November 2013 his baby daughter was born. In a clear sign that Jamie had resolved to keep his private life private, the news did not emerge until December. Nor was there any information about where she had been born – by that time Jamie was filming *Fifty Shades* in Vancouver – nor indeed what her name was, which at the time of writing has still not been made public.

He couldn't avoid the growing public attention, though. Jamie Dornan fansites were beginning to proliferate. There had been a few since his earliest modelling days, but now that Jamie was to play Christian Grey, many, many more sprang up in their place. He was papped absolutely everywhere. Lists of Jamie-related trivia began to appear. And so fans learned that his favourite books were *The Picture of Dorian Gray* by Oscar Wilde and *The Man in the Gray Flannel Suit* by Sloan Wilson, while his favourite author was Paul Auster. His favourite films were Disney's *Robin Hood* (a wise choice given his association with *Once Upon a Time*), alongside *Terminator*, *Die Hard* and *Annie Hall* – certainly an eclectic selection. Favourite actresses included Angelina Jolie and Diane Keaton, and favourite musicians included Nick Drake, Van Morrison, Neil Young, Crosby, Stills and Nash, Bob Dylan and KT Tunstall.

And that wasn't all. It emerged that Jamie suffered from asthma and was forced to keep an inhaler with him at all times. He didn't like horror films or tabloids (no surprise there), and as well as rugby, he enjoyed football, golf, tennis, skiing and sailing (possibly the secret to that physique). He supported Bangor Football Club, enjoyed folk music and barbecues, and his favourite city was New York. He was a big fan of Guinness, too, good Irish lad that he was. He liked hamburgers and he was capable of opening a beer bottle with his teeth.

Jamie was in fact now experiencing the kind of attention he had experienced second hand when he was dating Keira, and that early experience had clearly taught him how to cope. He was happy to give interviews – given the high-profile nature of his work, he could hardly do otherwise – but while revealing himself to be remarkably good-natured, he gave little away about his personal life. He was protecting Amelia and their daughter as best he could, as he was only too aware of how difficult being in the public eye could be.

Jamie's good nature was demonstrated wherever he went. He appeared on *The Graham Norton Show*, where he held his own against not only the spirited host, but also Ant and Dec and *Breaking Bad*'s Aaron Paul. Jamie had the audience in stitches as he talked about the fact that an old school chum had commented on his big calves – 'That wasn't all we talked about' – and the way he used to walk – 'The director said to me, "Is that a character thing?"' – revealing himself to be a genuinely likeable person. He even demonstrated his funny walk, telling the audience that it was Amelia who'd showed him that most people walked heel to toe, rather than toe and more toe. By laughing at himself, Jamie was not only keeping up with the other famously witty guests, he had the audience eating out of his hand.

His appearance on *Graham Norton* garnered a good deal of publicity, with people flocking to social media to comment on the fact that Jamie seemed like a genuine and nice fellow. He was funny and self-deprecating and a thoroughly decent man. No one appeared to have a bad word to say against him – indeed, the only time his name appeared in a slightly negative context was when a list appeared purporting to name the actress Lindsay Lohan's conquests and Jamie was on it, despite always denying any rumours that they had ever dated. (So, too, were Colin Farrell, Joaquin Phoenix, Zac Efron and various others.) But that was all in the past: Jamie was now happy, settled and a committed family man.

There were two themes that recurred constantly in interviews: the fear that people wouldn't take him seriously because he had started out as a model, which Jamie brought up over and over, and the downside of being on the receiving end of a huge amount of attention. One interviewer expressed concern, because whatever Jamie had experienced to date was going to be amplified a thousandfold when his next project hit the big screen. Jamie had once expressed the opinion that he was never going to be as famous as Keira, but with the prospect of him appearing in one of the most hotly anticipated films for decades, many thought otherwise. Jamie's life was about to shift up a gear once more.

13

Snowqueens Icedragon

Snowqueens Icedragon was hard at work. She had been writing her first novel, *Master of the Universe*, for some time now, posting online as she went and receiving comments, suggestions and hints from her readers. As polite as she was committed to her work, Icy, as she often signed herself, would never fail to thank them: 'Thanks to Songster51, ElleNathan & Rhian for a wonderful Saturday Night,' was one typical post, which went up on 20 November 2010. 'Thanks to Hoot – for pre-reading and checking my American. Thanks also to the twitterati for their continued help with the Amercian' [sic].

A fortnight later she was back: 'Wow . . . what an awesome response to the last chapter,' she typed. 'Thank you. Peeps unhappy at Bella or Edward – or both of them. Sheesh will these two get a break.'

Bella and Edward? Now those two names certainly rang a bell. For Bella Swan and Edward Cullen were the star-crossed young lovers at the centre of the *Twilight* series, the human girl and vampire boy who were madly in love with one another, but who had to be careful unless their passion made

Edward lose control of himself and accidentally kill her. The author of the series, Stephenie Meyer, was a practising Mormon and it has often been noted that hers is an excellent example of a tale advising teenagers to abstain from sex.

The *Twilight* series – both the books and subsequent films starring Kristen Stewart and Robert Pattinson, who only exacerbated the hysteria surrounding it all when they became a real-life couple – was an absolute sensation. People became obsessed with it, including Snowqueens Icedragon, who was writing her story on *FanFiction.Net*, a site that attracted writers (or more accurately, fans) who took characters that had already been created by someone else and wrote stories about them. Master of the Universe was even illustrated with pictures of Bella and Edward, so there wasn't too much doubt about who was the inspiration.

So who was she, this Snowqueens Icedragon? From the small amount of information she made known about herself, she certainly sounded a jolly sort. Revealing that she was married to a 'grumpy hubs', lived in west London and had two sons, she posted, 'I am old enough to know better, but will try anything once – except incest and folk dancing . . . actually I've tried folk dancing and it's a hoot . . .' She worked in television, she said, and more pertinently, 'I started writing in January 2009 after I finished the *Twilight* saga, and I haven't stopped since.' She invited contact on twitter@SQicedragon or at her full moniker on *Twilighted.net* and *FanFiction.net*.

These days @SQicedragon's tweets are protected and would-be followers have to ask permission to join the hallowed few (5,879 of them, to be more exact). By contrast another tweeter, E L James, has 557,000 followers, but everyone has to make a start. Meanwhile, Snowqueens Icedragon has vanished from *Twilighted.net*, and while she is still listed on *FanFiction.net*, there is no record of her work. Mystery? Well, not quite.

These days it is well known that the mysterious Snowqueens Icedragon is none other than E L James herself, the author of the monumentally successful *Fifty Shades of Grey* series, which has sold so massively that they have now overtaken the great Stephenie Meyer herself, and *Master of the Universe* was the first version of *Fifty Shades*. You'd be hard pressed to find any of the original now, though, despite the best efforts of netectives, because when *Fifty Shades'* commercial potential became clear, every trace of the original was wiped. No one has ever pretended that the stories started in any other way, but neither do they want to make a song and dance about it. *Fifty Shades* stands alone in its own right.

'This did start as *Twilight* fan fiction, inspired by Stephenie Meyer's wonderful series of books,' her agent Valerie Hoskins told *Deadline Hollywood*. 'Originally it was written as fan fiction, then Erika decided to take it down after there were some comments about the racy nature of the material. She took it down and thought, I'd always wanted to write. I've got a couple of unpublished novels here. I'll rewrite this thing and create these iconic characters, Christian and Ana.'

E L James, or Erica Leonard, née Mitchell, is an unlikely

candidate to have written a raunchy novel that catapulted her into mega-fame and huge wealth, to say nothing of being named as one of 'The World's Most Influential People' by *Time* magazine in 2012. Born on 2 March 1963 to a Chilean mother and Scottish father who worked for the BBC as a cameraman, Erica was brought up in Buckinghamshire and studied history at Kent University before becoming a studio manager's assistant at the National Film and Television School in Beaconsfield. In 1987 she married screenwriter and director Niall Leonard, who had worked on *Hornblower*, *Silent Witness* and *Wire in the Blood*, and she subsequently gave birth to two sons.

Apart from the fact that she worked in the slightly exotic field of television, becoming television producer for *Shooting Stars*, which was owned by Vic Reeves and Bob Mortimer, there was nothing to mark Erika out as a woman who would become a news story herself. Until the *Twilight* fascination began, she was a perfectly normal middle-class wife and mother, looking after the family and doing her best. Tweets after she became famous revealed a fondness for Oyster Bay sauvignon blanc, eating Nutella with a spoon and driving a Mini. But then, towards the end of 2008, she picked up the tale of Edward and Bella. Totally engrossed, almost as soon as she finished the quartet of novels she sat down to write.

The rest, as they say, is history. First *Master of the Universe* went up on the fansite, next, after fellow authors made comments to the effect that it was rather racy, Erica took it down and put it on her own website, *FiftyShades.com*. Contrary to popular myth, Erica did not self-publish the novels: rather, an Australian publisher, The Writer's Coffee Shop, saw the potential of the writing and published them as e-books and print-on-demand paperbacks.

What happened next astounded everyone, including Erica, and gave rise to phrases such as 'Mommy porn' and '*Twilight* for adults'. The books, now extensively reworked as a trilogy, came to the attention of Vintage Books, who snapped them up for a seven-figure sum. Despite the high-profile success stories of authors like J. K. Rowling, such a story is incredibly unusual in the world of publishing, especially for a complete unknown. But word of mouth continued to build the hype: first a new e-book of the trilogy appeared, followed by an announcement of a 750,000 print run at some considerable speed. Something was clearly afoot.

In the middle of all this, Erica watched, stunned, as what had started out as a little piece of fan fiction turned into the publishing event of the year. It seemed she was as taken aback as everyone else. 'I was amazed how popular it was. I'm still amazed,' she told Michelle Kosinski on NBC's *Today* show. And she was absolutely adamant about what lay behind the work: 'This is my midlife crisis writ large,' she said. The books were 'kind of raw' she admitted. And as for the dominant nature of the hero, of which more anon, would women really want that? she was asked. 'Once you're in charge of your job, your house, your children, getting the food on the table, doing all of this, all of the time, it'd be nice for someone else to be in charge for a bit maybe [but] in real life you want someone who does the dishes,' said Erica rather coyly.

It was, as she admitted over and over, fantasy, but fantasy that created shock waves. The book revolved around BDSM, after all – bondage, discipline, sadism and masochism – hardly the stuff of a vicar's tea party. And what was perhaps most amusing was that the people who seemed the most shocked were men. It seemed it had never occurred to the men of the world that as their womenfolk slaved away over a hot stove they might be dreaming of something a little more exciting, a man who looked like Christian/Jamie hurling them around in the bedroom, even if Christian's sexual tastes were a little too much for most. Men simply couldn't understand it: for the best part of forty years, they had been lectured at and told to find their feminine side. Admittedly, most did not, but even so, to find that the latest literary drool fest was a bloke with a Red Room of Pain and a penchant for whips was a little bit much.

Indeed, such was the shock and sensation around what Erica had written that it opened up a debate on its own: was this what women really wanted? Christian, after all, wants to physically hurt Ana: could it be OK for someone to write about this, implying that all women want to be dominated? (It should be noted that Christian persistently tries to get Ana to sign a dominance contract and she point-blank refuses, so she's not quite the pushover she's sometimes made out to be.) But a woman had written this and women, in their millions, were reading it. What did that say about us all?

To Erica, who after all should know, the real appeal of the book lay in the fact that it was, at its heart, a love story. 'No, it's the love story. Women like to read a passionate love story,' she said while making an appearance at an event to promote *Fifty Shades of Grey: The Classical Album*, a tie-in featuring music that inspired her, including Chopin and Debussy (marketing opportunities were coming in thick and fast now). 'There is sex, but as the books go on, the sex changes as the relationship changes. You see the evolution of it. Women of all ages are reading it – from women at university right through to women in their nineties. I get the most TMI [too much information] emails you could ever hope for. People go and try this stuff.

'I hope teenagers aren't reading it, but I think a few are because I get emails from them as well, and I wish they weren't.'

One of the many jokes doing the rounds about lady readers' new-found taste for titillation is that they could read it on their Kindle and no one would know. Erica agreed that this had helped. 'E-readers have been very liberating for people because they can read whatever they like with no judgment,' she said. 'In fact, I designed the book covers because in my early thirties I read a lot of romantic fiction when I was slogging into and out of London on the Tube, and they had these horrible covers with women with their clothes falling off.

I hated that, so I designed discreet covers where nobody would know it's a really salacious novel.' Never mind the fact that 30 per cent of *Fifty Shades* readers turned out to be men.

Accolades of a sort came thick and fast. Erica had had to put up with a great deal of stick about her slightly pedestrian writing style, but who cared now that she was so seriously rich. Then, in April 2012, came *Time*'s 100 most influential list: 'Six months ago she was Erika Leonard, a mother of two who dabbled in saucy stories for the web,' it said. 'Now she's E L James, publishing phenomenon, whose *Fifty Shades of Grey* trilogy has deeply stirred booksellers, Hollywood and, apparently, many, many mothers. Reading may never be the same.'

That might have been overstating it a little, but there was no doubt Erika had touched a chord. Feathers were ruffled once more when US *Publishers Weekly* named her as its 'publishing person of the year', citing the fact that she had made naughty books 'hot'. 'Because the success of the series continues to reverberate throughout the industry in a number of ways – among other things, the money it's brought in helped boost print sales in bookstores and turned erotic fiction into a hot category – we have selected James as the most notable player on the publishing stage this year,' it said.

This really upset purists. For a start, the award had never gone to an author before; it had always gone to someone in the publishing industry. The *Los Angeles Times* said, 'What was *Publishers Weekly* thinking? James wrote fan fiction, she got it independently published by a micro e-press, it went viral, she got a book deal, she started collecting serious paychecks. All that is great news for an individual author, but it hardly justifies making that individual the Publishing Person of the Year . . . It's really impossible to say that James has done much more than get very, very lucky, although *PW* tries to make that case. Someone who stumbles across a jackpot is certainly fortunate, but should they be anointed with an industry's laurels? Maybe someday *PW* will find a person in publishing who is doing something, rather than having something done to them, and name the individual Publishing Person of the Year.'

Poor Erika. Even the comments on the *Publishers Weekly* website were livid. 'I want to die. Or kill. Or just eat some cake until this literary pain goes away.' 'Seriously? Is this the best you guys can do? Hilary Mantel becomes the first woman to win the Booker Prize twice and you pick E L James? Lay off the eggnog and rethink your decision.' If it was any consolation, Erika was crying all the way to the bank. As the millions continued to role in, she was spotted looking at agreeable country mansions. Home until then had been a considerably humbler semi-detached in Ealing – not London's flashiest post code.

Then it was announced that the film rights had sold for $5 million. Angelina Jolie or Scarlett Johansson were both wrongly predicted to play the female lead. By this time it had been translated into forty languages, and such was the hysteria surrounding the books that a baby boom was predicted on the back of a crazed generation of women demanding their husbands turn into their own version of Christian Grey.

Erika herself, although now looking considerably more groomed than when she'd first entered the public arena, on the whole kept in the background, while her husband was the subject of much lascivious conjecture about what it must be like to be married to a woman like Erika. Her teenage sons hadn't read it, Erica revealed, adding that they would be 'mortified'. So what was this book that had made such an astonishing impact? What was the story it told?

Because of the hero's interesting personal proclivities, it is often thought that *Fifty Shades of Grey* is essentially smut with a story tacked on. Actually, it's the other way around. As Erika herself points out, *Fifty Shades* is essentially a love story, and if you take out the whips element, it features a hero who fits right in there with Messrs Darcy, Rochester, et al. The story starts with Anastasia Steele, known as Ana, a twenty-one-year-old student at Washington State University in Vancouver, who works on the student newspaper. Her friend and fellow journalist Kate is supposed to be interviewing the enigmatic businessman Christian Grey, who despite being only twenty-seven is already a billionaire, but she is ill. Ana goes to the interview in her stead, and the attraction between her and Grey is immediate.

It's soon clear to the reader, if not to Ana, where this is heading. Christian turns up at the hardware store where Ana works and, an early indication of his interesting personal tastes, buys some masking tape and rope, while giving Ana his number. They arrange a photo session with Ana's friend José, go for coffee and learn that they are both single. Ana then goes to a party, gets drunk and calls Christian, who comes to collect her; she wakes up the next morning in his hotel room, although he has been the perfect gentleman. He informs her he would like to take things further, but somewhat unusually wants her to sign a non-disclosure agreement. This leads to a date where Christian flies her in his helicopter to his apartment in Seattle. There he shows her his Red Room of Pain, essentially an S&M torture chamber, before discovering she is a virgin (shades of the late Barbara Cartland couldn't have been stronger here) and relieving her of her virginity. However, he now wants her to sign a second contract, in which she will agree to be dominated by him and will also agree that the relationship is only a sexual one, not a romantic one. Something most commentators tend to miss here is that Ana never actually signs this contract.

And so starts a cat-and-mouse game in which Ana gets scared and runs away, Christian hauls her back in again, spanks her and introduces her to his family, as you do. It's revealed that he lost his own virginity aged fifteen to a friend of his mother's, which is where he developed a taste for S&M, and although he continues to insist she must sign the contract and that they are not having a relationship, it is clear that that's exactly what is developing between them. Ana somewhat conveniently gets a job at Seattle Independent Publishing, gets spanked some more and then, after Christian goes too far and beats her with a belt, she leaves him for good. Or does she? Whatever the case, the book ends here.

Many authors of populist fiction are torn apart by the

critics, and it wasn't long before Erika learned that they can be just as cruel as Christian on a bad day. Sir Salman Rushdie, who has never, even in his wildest dreams, achieved anything like the sales Erika was enjoying said, 'I've never read anything so badly written that got published. It made *Twilight* look like *War and Peace*.' Interesting that he had clearly read *Twilight*, though.

Maureen Dowd in *The New York Times* said it was 'like a Brontë devoid of talent', adding that it was 'dull and poorly written'. Jesse Kornbluth of *The Huffington Post* said, 'As a reading experience, *Fifty Shades* . . . is a sad joke, puny of plot.'

No one, Erika included, could have claimed the book was great literature, but it was compelling, a page-turner and, given the sales, it clearly meant something to the millions of readers who couldn't put it down. Some people were astute enough to realize that, too. 'Though no literary masterpiece, *Fifty Shades* is more than parasitic fan fiction based on the recent *Twilight* vampire series,' said Princeton professor April Alliston. Jenny Colgan, herself a bestselling populist author, wrote in the *Guardian*, 'It is jolly, eminently readable and as sweet and safe as BDSM (bondage, discipline, sadism and masochism) erotica can be without contravening the trade descriptions act' and, crucially perhaps, 'more enjoyable' than other 'literary erotic books'.

The *Daily Telegraph* said it was a 'treacly cliché', but added that it would have female readers 'discussing it for years to come'. A reviewer for the *Ledger-Enquirer* pointed out that it 'also touches on one aspect of female existence [female sub-mission]. And acknowledging that fact – maybe even appreciating it – shouldn't be a cause for guilt.'

The *New Zealand Herald* said it 'will win no prizes for its prose' and 'there are some exceedingly awful descriptions', but if you 'can suspend your disbelief and your desire to – if you'll pardon the expression – slap the heroine for having so little self-respect, you might enjoy it'.

The *Columbus Dispatch* said, 'Despite the clunky prose, James does cause one to turn the page.' *Metro News Canada* felt that 'suffering through 500 pages of this heroine's inner dialogue was torturous, and not in the intended, sexy kind of way'. Jessica Reaves, of the *Chicago Tribune*, wrote that the 'book's source material isn't great literature', it was, 'sprinkled liberally and repeatedly with asinine phrases', and was 'depressing'.

Despite all that, in December 2012, it won both the Popular Fiction and Book of the Year categories in the UK National Book Awards.

The criticism, and there was an awful lot of it, was based primarily on three things: the fact that its origins lay in fan fiction, that it glamorized BDSM and that the prose wasn't entirely up there with Shakespeare. Regarding the first of these, did it really matter? By the time *Fifty Shades* had appeared, no one would have made the association with *Twilight* had they not already known about it – the new work had taken on a life and character of its own. Christian and Ana were nothing like Edward and Bella, and this certainly wouldn't have been the first time a work of art was inspired by something that already exists.

The depiction of BDSM was more problematic, inspiring some very high-powered ladies to get involved in the debate. Katie Roiphe of *Newsweek* wrote, 'But why, for women especially, would free will be a burden? . . . It may be that power is not always that comfortable, even for those of us who grew up in it; it may be that equality is something we want only sometimes and in some places and in some arenas; it may be that power and all of its imperatives can be boring.'

There were many high-powered ladies of the opinion that a little BDSM was no bad thing. *Zap2it*'s Andrea Reiher snapped, 'being submissive sexually is not tantamount to being the victim of abuse' or 'giving up their power or their equality with their partner'. The Jezebel website was closest to the mark when it said, 'The vast majority of fans fawn over the emotional relationship Anastasia and Christian have, not about the sex.'

Not to be outdone, *Salon.com* interviewed several dominatrices, including Melissa Febos, who said that even if it demonstrated 'current anxieties about equality' it 'doesn't mean that it's evidence of unhappiness, or an invalidation of feminism'. Instead, she argued, it might actually be a sign of progress that millions of women are so hungrily pursuing sexual fantasies independently of men.

In the midst of this discussion, however, it should be pointed out that Christian and Ana's is a consensual relationship the whole way through. Meanwhile institutions were getting in on the act too: public libraries in Brevard County, Florida, had the book removed from its shelves due to the 'sexual content', only for them to cave in and reinstate them due to popular demand. In Macaé, Brazil, a judge ruled that bookstores should either remove the books or hide them; his comments came after he saw children reading them. There was a huge row when the pornographic film-makers Smash Pictures said that it was going to film an adult version of the story called *Fifty Shades of Grey: A XXX Adaptation*: Universal had already bought the film rights to the book and sued them. Smash Pictures then countersued and the matter was eventually settled out of court.

Erika, whose bank account was growing by the minute, watched all this in disbelief. Never in her wildest dreams had she, or anyone else for that matter, expected such an outcome from a little fan worship, and as the frenzy surrounding who would play Christian built, everything seemed entirely unreal. Whatever the naysayers came up with, there was no escaping the fact that Erika had created something that women all over the world could relate to. Now there was just the minor matter of portraying the whole thing on film.

14

Mr Grey Will See
You Now

E L James was in a very good place. Not only was she earning millions through her bestselling novel, but the biggest film companies in the world were queuing up to buy the film rights. Warner Bros, Sony, Paramount, Universal and even Mark Wahlberg's production company were bidding for it, and Wahlberg came closer than you might think. 'We were very close to getting the rights; we were talking with the writer before she had an agent,' he told *yahoo.com*. 'I just knew that it was going to be a phenomenon, whether I thought it was good, bad or indifferent. It was definitely going to be one of those things that would create a huge buzz.'

He was certainly right there. Had any book ever produced a bigger buzz? Eventually Universal and Focus Features won the battle in March 2012, with Erika maintaining some considerable control over the film process. The $40 million production was now under way. Michael De Luca and Dana Brunetti, who had worked on *The Social Network*, were brought on board as producers – by all accounts at Erika's request – and the hunt for a director began. This was as important as finding the right star and various names came up, including Joe Wright, Patty Jenkins, Bill Condon, Bennett Miller and Steven Soderburgh. Eventually, in June 2013, well over a year after they'd bought the rights, it was announced that Sam Taylor-Johnson, a photographer and member of the Young British Artists group that included Damian Hirst, had landed the role. It was a surprise choice, and proof that Universal didn't just want something steamy; they were going for something much more sophisticated instead.

Next up was the scriptwriter. Bret Easton Ellis threw his hat in the ring, but wasn't successful, and in the end a number of people became involved, including Kelly Marcel, Patrick Marber and Mark Bomback. This in turn gave rise to rumours that there was some concern over the script, but in fact, the hiring of Marber, whose past work included *Closer* and *Notes on a Scandal*, and who had previously worked with Taylor-Johnson, was standard practice, and it was more likely that eyebrows were raised because his arrival more or less coincided with Charlie Hunnam's departure. On such a high-profile project every small change was bound to cast wider ripples than it would normally have done.

The circumstances surrounding the casting of Jamie have already been covered, but the initial announcement, that the two stars would be Charlie and Dakota Johnson, was made at the beginning of September 2013, though Charlie was replaced with Jamie shortly afterwards. Meanwhile Dakota had been up against stiff competition for the role of Ana, with other contenders including Alicia Vikander, Imogen Poots, Elizabeth Olsen, Shailene Woodley and Felicity Jones.

Keira's name also came up in early deliberations, before Jamie was involved in the project, but she was quick to rule herself out. When asked about Jamie getting the role she laughed and replied, 'Well he's a very good-looking boy. I'm sure the girls will love him.' Charlie also gave him the thumbs up: 'I don't know him personally, but I'm sure he will do a great job,' he told the *Daily Mirror*. 'I don't really know his work but I know Sam, the director's, is amazing. And she has fantastic taste, so I am sure that he is going to do a great job.' Yet another admirer was the Irish actress Aisling Franciosi, who played the predatory babysitter Katie in *The Fall*. 'I can see looks-wise why he has been cast and I think he proved that he earned his acting stripes on *The Fall*,' she told the *Daily Mirror*. 'He had done a lot of modelling as well. I know there were some people who were sceptical, but I think he proved them all wrong and people are singing his praises.'

Dakota was also a surprise choice for some. Born on 4 October 1989 to actors Don Johnson and Melanie Griffiths, her family was part of the Hollywood establishment. Her grandparents were Tippi Hedren and Peter Griffith, a child star turned advertising executive, her half-aunt is the actress Tracy Griffith, and for many years, until he recently separated from her mother, her stepfather was Antonio Banderas. Dakota grew up in Colorado and LA and studied dance as a child; her film debut came in 1999 when she and her half-sister Stella Banderas appeared in *Crazy in Alabama* alongside their mother, with Antonio directing. 'My dad was doing *Nash Bridges* in San Francisco, so I was there, like, every day,' she told *Elle*. 'My mom was doing a bunch of stuff, still making movies, and Antonio was making movies. I was everywhere, all over the world. I loved it so much.' She launched herself as an actress proper, and subsequent films included small parts in *The Social Network*, *Beastly*, *For Ellen* and various others. In 2006 she was voted Miss Golden Globes, the first ever second-generation Miss Golden Globes in the award's history.

But despite that, Dakota was still something of an unknown, and she had never played the lead in a high-profile film. There was surprise and disquiet from some quarters about the casting, but no one, other than those involved, was really in a position to judge her suitability for the role. In some ways, had a higher-profile and better-known name been cast, the identity of the actress might have overshad-owed the role she was playing. Anastasia was, after all, supposed to be a naive ingénue: to take a little-known actress for the role meant that there would be no preconceptions as to how she would come across. 'I really understand it,' Dakota told the *Daily Mirror*. 'I think it's an incredible love story and that's why it's affected so many people. Erika did a good job of explaining how that can happen and you have this chemical pull to someone. Adding in the sex makes it perfect. Sometimes you feel a little bit naughty and that's OK.'

There was, however, some very amused speculation as to how her father, who'd been something of a ladies' man in his heyday, would react. 'This is the family business,' he told *Good Morning Britain* in the summer of 2014. 'This is what we do, and I am absolutely certain that Dakota will take a piece of material and a character which a lot of people might imagine could be inappropriate in some ways and turn it into something spectacular. Speaking like a proud father and a seasoned professional, I can tell you that she is a gifted, gifted actress and this will just be one part in a long line of tremendous performances in her career.'

However, he did go on to tell the *Daily Telegraph*, 'I probably will not see it just because it's not a movie I would see. I've never seen *The Vampire Diaries*, I've never seen *Twilight*. It's in a category of films that I just wouldn't be interested in.' It was probably a wise decision, and Dakota was certainly relieved, pointing out that if her parents were appearing in a steamy film, she wouldn't want to see it either.

In many ways both lead actors were relative unknowns – Jamie had not broken the States – which the producers thought was to their advantage. 'No matter who we cast, people were gonna be angry about it. And then we obviously had the one that we cast that ultimately didn't work out,' said Dana Brunetti. 'We have to meet the ideas of the fans to an extent and make them happy – although you're not gonna make them happy as they're thinking of somebody else in their mind. I always thought it would be better if we went with somebody unknown so everyone can discover them together, that's where I really think we are now with Jamie and Dakota.'

In time the rest of the cast was announced. Victor Rasuk was to play José Rodriguez Jr, Eloise Mumford was Kate Kavanagh, the singer Rita Ora was Christian's younger sister Mia and Marcia Gay Harden was Christian's mother Grace.

But, of course, the real focus of attention was on the two leads. How were they going to put the story across and cope with the subject matter? Neither seemed particularly phased. 'I'm a fairly liberal guy, I grew up in a very liberal place,' Jamie told *Entertainment Weekly*. 'I'm not saying we had a play-room but I'm not shocked by the sex in the book. It's essential to tell the story. I can't believe films that don't invoke the sexual side of it. So it works for me.' This was just as well, as any coyness about the material would have been a disaster.

The book was set in Seattle (which E L James has famously never visited), but filming was to take place in Vancouver, with the Gastown area of the city providing the backdrop for many of the major scenes. The University of British Columbia stood in for Washington State University Vancouver, and the Fairmont Hotel Vancouver was The Heathman Hotel. After several delays, filming started in late November 2013 and finished the following February. Initially there were plans to release the movie in the summer of 2014, but this was pushed back to the more suitable date of 14 February 2015, Valentine's Day. There was, however, a debate about how explicit the film should be. The producers didn't want an X rating as that would significantly limit the prospective audience, but neither did they want to be too cautious. In the end it was announced that the film would be an R, which means it's viewable by anyone who is seventeen or over in the United States.

Dana Brunetti, incidentally, had a novel solution: to produce two versions of the film. 'Everybody could go and enjoy the 15s version, and then if they really wanted to see it again and get a little bit more gritty with it then have that 18s version out there as well,' he told the *Daily Mirror*. 'It'd be great for the studio, too, because they'd get a double dip on the box office. What we're kind of hearing from the fans is they want it dirty. They want it as close as possible to the book. We want to keep it elevated but also give the fans what they want.' In the end everyone involved managed to toe a difficult line: it was rumoured that some of the scenes were dropped as they were just too raunchy and the film-makers went for the broadest appeal. When filming the sex scenes, as is usual in the industry, the director, Sam, cleared the set to have the minimum number of people necessary present, which in this case proved to be twelve.

One advantage to pushing back the release date was that it gave the producers plenty of time to mount a publicity campaign and the full force of the marketing team swung into action. In January 2014, around the time that filming was wrapped up, Universal released a poster of Jamie, clad in a suit, gazing moodily out of floor-to-ceiling windows, looking down on Vancouver/Seattle, with the caption 'Mr Grey Will See You Now' – a line the receptionist gives Ana when she first goes to interview him. This was almost unprecedented, given that the opening of the film was more than a year away, but the producers clearly intended to ramp up interest in the film early by teasing the audience, if you will.

A good deal of thought had gone into how Christian would come across, with Jamie and Sam Taylor-Johnson working it out between them. 'I think there was so much more to Christian than we covered – someone who is careful to keep himself in shape, someone who spends obscene amounts of money on presenting himself,' Jamie told *Interview* magazine. 'A lot of that work was done in the gym and with costume. We didn't talk about particulars of the way he would move. But I'm quite awkward in a suit because I don't have an opportunity to wear one very often, and this is a guy who lives in a suit – the best suit. That has to have an effect. But when you end up in a suit for 80 per cent of the filming process, you become pretty comfortable with it.' It was an unusual concern; most actors are more concerned about dealing with nudity – another requirement for the role. But for all Jamie's angst about his modelling career, it had made him very comfortable about displaying his body.

As time wore on, glimpses of the two on set provoked near feverish excitement, with much speculation about how good the chemistry between them was. Headline writers had a field day: 'Kisstian Grey', they yelled. 'Dornan and Dirty'. 'Grey-t news girls'. 'Nifty Shades of Jay'. When Dakota and Jamie were seen having a cup of tea together the inevitable headline was, 'Fifty Shades of Earl Grey'. And when a long profile of Jamie appeared in *The Sunday Times* it was accompanied by the headline, 'The Golden Torso With the Whip Hand'.

Robert Johnston, associate editor of *GQ*, was quoted in the profile as saying, 'He has acting ability. Also, obviously, he's got a good agent. Normally pretty boys wouldn't be put forward for that kind of part [Paul Spector] because they worry, "Oh, people will think I'm nasty."' The secret to Jamie's success, he said, was that he had a strong personality. 'Without wanting to sound rude about models, that's slightly unusual,' he continued. 'The reason most models don't successfully turn into actors is they don't tend to have great personalities. People who are terribly good looking often aren't very interesting. Dornan has got something.'

Both Jamie and Dakota were having to prepare themselves for a massive publicity campaign and an accompanying level of attention that neither had experienced before. Both had seen it at second hand – Jamie through Keira and Dakota through her parents – but nothing could prepare them for what was going to happen, no matter how much they'd been warned. 'I have no idea how it's going to go,' Dakota told *Elle*. 'I plan on handling it gracefully, to live my life as close as I can to how I do now.' That was really the only practicable way forward, and in Dakota's case she had seen how private troubles turned into public ones, as her parents' past problems had a history of making the front page. Robert Pattinson, who experienced the same thing when the *Twilight* films came out, later commented that initially the loss of freedom was hard to take, but eventually he became so used to the attention that he hardly noticed it. That was the road Jamie and Dakota were now going down.

Like Jamie, Dakota was relaxed about the subject matter. 'I think women should pursue whatever kind of relationship they want and makes them happy, and if that's S&M, that's great,' she told *Elle*. 'I don't have any problem doing anything. The secret is I have no shame.' She was laughing at herself but that wasn't entirely true – not for the first time, she also spoke publicly about the fact that she didn't want her parents to see the film. She was probably safe on that one, though, as they didn't want to see it either.

Like Jamie, Dakota had thought about the character she would be playing. 'I just thought Ana was a real girl,' she said. 'There's nothing fake or phony about her, and I appreciate that. She's goofy and she's smart and she's pretty normal. Reading the book, I found myself more interested in the ways they were breaking each other down emotionally than the sex scenes. I think there's a part of a woman that wants to be the thing that breaks a man down. I wasn't very invested at first, just because I was a little scared of it. The material was intense, and I've never done anything like that before. But that just told me it was something I should do.'

Dakota was quite right in that what really fuelled the popularity of *Fifty Shades of Grey* was not the sex but that it was a love story. Christian was part of the tradition of the troubled hero rescued by the love of an ingénue. That was really the key to the book's popularity, and it was also probably the reason why Sam had been brought in as the director. The producers didn't want smut; they wanted a love story – with a certain amount of steaminess thrown in.

Jamie continued to strive to keep his feet on the ground. It would have been easy to let it all go to his head at that stage, but he was determined to remain the level-headed fellow he had always been. 'I despise extravagance,' he said in an interview with Polish *Glamour*. 'I do not fly a private plane. I do not have bodyguards and I do not buy branded stuff. I have a house, two dogs, a watch. That's good enough for me. I'm a thirty-one-year-old, not twenty-one. I don't leave clubs at 5 a.m. Who would be interested in a nerd like me? Honestly, when I hear that I'm cute and charming, I feel like a French bulldog. You can become a conceited arsehole or do something good for the world, the latter being much more difficult. I don't try to be cool or trendy. I'm an individualist. Mostly in life I want to be myself.' That wasn't going to be a problem, but it didn't alleviate the intense interest in everything he did. It was commendable that he was making an effort to remain untouched by it all, but Jamie was a genuine A-lister now and people were bound to treat him as such.

On 14 February 2014, a year before the film came out, a still of Dakota as Anastasia appeared. In June, a still of Jamie appeared, in honour of Christian's birthday. Then E L James got in on the act, announcing via Twitter that the film's trailer would be appearing in July. Beyoncé, who had recorded a new version of 'Crazy In Love', her massively successful single, for the film, which also featured in the trailer, put out a teaser on her Instagram account, and then the trailer duly appeared.

Jamie and Dakota appeared together on the *Today* show to

present the trailer, which had been heavily edited for morning television viewing (steamier scenes were released later in the day). The publicity department was doing a splendid job, and as a sign of the massive interest in the film the trailer resulted in 36.4 million hits in the first week, propelling it to the most viewed video on YouTube in 2014, with over 100 million hits. Twitter was reporting 98,000 mentions of *Fifty Shades* per hour while the frenzy was at its peak. And this was just a three-minute clip.

Meanwhile, it emerged that the book had now sold over 100 million copies all over the world and been translated into fifty-one languages, with further interest being fuelled by the forthcoming film. 'Guys, thank you for this,' tweeted E L James, as well she might. 'Thank you, thank you, thank you.' There had also been a huge boost in the sales of massage oils and adult toys, all attributed to the *Fifty Shades* effect.

Jamie and Dakota came across well on the *Today* show, where they were interviewed by Savannah Guthrie who, much to the disappointment of some fans, assured Jamie she wouldn't be asking him to take his top off. 'I could have done that if you asked me. I would have thought about it,' came the amiable response.

Dakota admitted that it had been a little intimidating undertaking the project. 'It's not like a romantic situation,' she said. 'It's more like technical and choreographed – it's like more of a task.'

'Wow,' said Jamie, pretending to look hurt.

Did they have chemistry he was asked. 'I presume we did

because they made that happen,' he said. 'And we had trust. We got ourselves into situations that were not that natural and not that easy and you had to have trust.' None of this did anything to dampen speculation about what was shaping up to be the hottest film for years.

The trailer continued to be popular. '*Fifty Shades of Grey* trailers are pulling monumental views,' said RelishMix CEO Marc Krazen to *The Escapist*. 'Add to that ripped and reposted versions on movie fan channels. It's unprecedented for a film that's six months out.' Indeed, fears that the film would bomb were looking pretty unlikely: if the trailer alone got that kind of attention, what would happen when the full-length version came out?

The book and the film were now so popular, completely unrelated celebrities were getting in on the act. 'Whips and chains are not my style, but who doesn't enjoy a jolly good spanking once in a while?' the actress Dame Helen Mirren asked innocently on *The Tonight Show*.

The singer and actress Lucy Hale revealed she'd auditioned for the role of Anastasia, and her description of the audition helped portray a salacious picture of what was going to happen on screen. 'That audition was so uncomfortable!' she told *Fox News*. 'It's exactly what you thought it would be: a big monologue but very, very sexual . . . there were some things that I was so embarrassed to be reading out loud, but it's one of those things where you have to commit wholeheartedly or you're going to make a fool of yourself.' Blimey. Whatever had they asked her to do?

More excitement followed. It was reported and then denied that the Philippines would ban the film, although it would have to be heavily toned down. Hotels began offering *Fifty Shades*-themed weekends away. Jamie shot to the top of the Internet Movie Database STARmeter rankings, meaning he was the most searched for star on IMDB, which boasts 190 million users a month. 'There is obviously some pent-up anticipation for this film,' said IMDB managing editor Keith Simanton with commendable understatement. A parody of the trailer appeared, in which the lead roles were acted out by dogs. Dakota took on another steamy role, in a film called *A Bigger Splash*, a remake of the French film *La Piscine*, co-starring alongside Tilda Swinton and Ralph Fiennes, an actor known for various steamy roles. And so the list continued.

Filming on *Fifty Shades* was now complete, and they just had to wait for the release. Jamie and everyone else involved on the film knew they'd been working on an extremely highly anticipated movie, and one that was likely to make a huge impact around the world. Meanwhile both Jamie and Dakota had started on new projects, so they'd only be reunited when publicity shoots were required and when the round of premieres began.

Jamie had done it, beaten off worldwide competition for one of the most sought-after roles in recent memory, climbing his way to the top of the A-list ladder in the process. Now it was back to real life and back to Blighty. There was more work to be done.

15

A Man in Much Demand

Well before Jamie landed the role of Christian Grey, it had been known that he would return to *The Fall* for a second series and that was what happened next. In early 2014 he headed back to Belfast: 'I'm delighted to be back in production for *The Fall*,' he told the *Daily Mirror*. 'Allan Cubitt has outdone himself and the scripts are stunning.' Gillian added, 'I'm over the moon to be back for what promises to be an even darker second season,' she said.

In the meantime, *Once Upon a Time* had become available on Sky On Demand, and, somewhat ironically given his early departure, Jamie's involvement was emphasized as one of its selling points.

Insistent that he didn't want to be famous for fame's sake, Jamie still sought to remain an ordinary guy. The *Daily Mail* asked how he was coping with the changes over the last year. 'In terms of professionally doing a job that's well received, it helps, but otherwise nothing's changed,' he said. 'I don't get recognized much, except when somebody shouted, "There's that serial killer!" at me – which provoked an interesting reaction. *The Fall* has changed the landscape of my professional career slightly, but I know so many actors who don't work and a few who work a lot. I'm just happy to do good work.'

Professional recognition was starting to come his way as well. In April 2014 the IFTA – Irish Film and Television Academy – awards were handed out and Jamie won two, as Best TV Actor for *The Fall* and for Rising Star. He was nominated for a Bafta for Best Actor in *The Fall*, too, although he didn't manage to bag that one. He was still managing to laugh at himself, though: 'I'd like to do a job where I don't have to tie women to beds,' he remarked. 'There are a couple of knots I know now and I've put them to good use far too many times recently.'

He wasn't beyond teasing his fans, either. Jamie had an Instagram account and used it to post a still from *Fifty Shades* in which he was pictured wearing boxer shorts standing over Dakota, who is kneeling and wearing a blindfold. 'You like?' he asked and got an overwhelmingly positive response – there was no denying the anticipation building in advance of the film. Jamie also came in at number eight on *Heat* magazine's Hottest Hunk list, the only Irishman to do so (Zac Efron came in at number one). Meanwhile, he continued to charm everyone he spoke to. When greeted outside the Baftas ceremony and congratulated on his first nomination, he bashfully (and inaccurately) protested that it would probably be his last. Asked whether *The Fall* or *Fifty Shades* had had the bigger impact on his life, he replied that he didn't know as

Fifty Shades hadn't yet been released. It was hard not to notice a tinge of nervousness about his demeanour. Jamie's life had already changed completely, and a great deal more upheaval was on the cards. 'I think I could lose my mind,' he said in another interview with the *Guardian*. That was partly down to exhaustion, but also to what Jamie perceived as an insane reaction to the news that he was to play the role of Christian Grey.

In April 2014 another little curiosity involving Jamie emerged, a film called *Flying Home*, which had been made in 2012 and was released only to cinemas in Belgium, although it found a wider audience on DVD. Directed by the Belgian film great Dominique Deruddere, it involved a rich young corporate raider living in New York, called Colin, whose life revolves totally around his work. Then he visits Flanders, where he tries to buy a champion pigeon for a potential client, a rich Arab sheikh, in return for the sheikh signing on with his company. In Flanders he pretends to be a teacher looking for the grave of his great grandfather, who died in the Great War, but then he meets Jos, the pigeon's owner and, more to the point, Isabelle (Charlotte De Bruyne), Jos's granddaughter, and complications ensue. The film also starred Anthony Head as Colin's father. It provoked a flurry of interest from Jamie's rapidly growing fan base, who were dismayed that it wasn't on in cinemas in the UK.

'The actor we wanted for the role of Colin had to be someone that would be able to portray in a believable way the reversal of a ruthless businessman, who encounters himself in Flanders fields and questions his lifestyle,' the director Dominique said on the film's website. 'I received a lot of resumés and tapes sent by young actors who fitted the picture "handsome and successful", but no one appeared to have that "second layer", which is so necessary for the main character. Jamie had subcutaneously more than his "pretty boy" look at first revealed. I was immediately interested and a scene from the yet unfinished *The Fall* . . . was decisive to me. This young fashion model turned out to be a solid actor! Jamie has managed to convey the increasing doubt and struggle of the main character with a lot of nuance and talent. He's an actor of whom we – of course also by his part in *Fifty Shades of Grey* – will hear a lot in the future worldwide.'

Jamie gave an interview to the Belgian Cobra website, bashfully admitting that he didn't speak Flemish (before trying out a few words). He found the film heartfelt and a little bit European, he added, and when his character was finally called upon to choose between right and wrong, he chose what was right. 'I liked the script and I love Dominic,' he added, a sentiment that was clearly reciprocated.

All in all, the general response was that this was a charming little offering and for various reasons, the timing could not have been better. 'This classically concocted melodrama is noteworthy mainly because it offers former Calvin Klein model and future *Fifty Shades of Grey* star Jamie Dornan his first romantic lead role, which should be enough to attract the interest of smart niche distributors who could time the film's release to coincide with the avalanche of publicity that Dornan's involvement in *Grey* is bound to generate. In its native Flanders, it made a tidy if not spectacular $500,000 when it was released last April,' wrote Boyd van Hoeij in the *Hollywood Reporter*, before going on to give it a favourable review. The consensus said very much the same.

Meanwhile, Jamie's much-maligned modelling career continued: in 2014, Jamie starred in the Ermenegildo Zegna couture spring ad campaign. But a subtle shift had occurred. Previously, Jamie had been a model who wanted to break into acting. Now he had become an actor who occasionally modelled. His change of status was complete.

He also started to sign up for new projects, first a film initially called *Chef* but then retitled *Adam Jones*. This boasted some seriously big names: Bradley Cooper as the chef, Uma Thurman, Emma Thompson, Sienna Miller and Lily James to name but a few. It was written by Steven Knight, and directed by John Wells. It was also a comedy, which was a genre Jamie had been saying he wanted to try for some time – he clearly needed a break from the trauma and angst of the roles he'd recently taken on. Full plot details were not made public, but it was known to feature a chef who had been out of the kitchen for some years after self-destructing in Paris, and who visited London in an effort to gain a third Michelin star. Cast members, including Jamie, were spotted in Marcus Wareing's two-starred restaurant in Knightsbridge. It certainly sounded like a very different movie to anything he'd done before, and his motivation for taking it may well have been a bid to avoid typecasting, although in truth it sounded like the ideal part for a young actor.

After that, Jamie signed up to play the lead in *The Siege of Jadotville*, an Irish action film about the siege of 150 UN Irish troops in the Congo in 1961, holding out against 3,000 local troops, led by French and Belgian mercenaries. They were led by Commandant Pat Quinlan, who Jamie was to play, during the turmoil created when Moise Tshombe killed the Congolese leader Patrice Lumumba and took control of the Katanga region. The director was Richie Smyth and filming was due to begin after the premiere of *Fifty Shades of Grey*, with filming split between Ireland and South Africa. 'I can't wait to get stuck into *Jadotville*,' Jamie told the *Irish Independent*. 'It's an unbelievable story and Commandant Pat Quinlan is going to be a treat of a character to tackle. I'm a big fan of both Richie Smyth and Alan Moloney and I'm very much looking forward to working with them both.'

As is so often the way, once you're in demand, everyone wants a piece of you. And many of the cast members of *Once Upon a Time* seemed to regret the loss of their handsome Hunter, sending fond little messages out into the ether in the hope of getting him back. 'We're still good friends and obviously Jamie has quite the schedule,' Emma/Jennifer Morrison told *E!* 'But we're hoping that someday there will be a moment when he's available to come back and reprise some flashbacks of Sheriff Graham.' It was unlikely, though. Now that the world was starting to open up for Jamie, why would he want to go back to a programme that was in his past?

Jennifer had happy memories of filming with Jamie. 'We had a great time together,' she recalled. 'One of the many things that Adam and Eddy had done an incredible job with is casting people with chemistry. I loved working with Jamie, I loved working with Michael Raymond-James, I love working with Colin. We all had chemistry in different ways, but in three very effective ways . . . So you know, Jamie and I had a great time and he's been tragically missed from the moment that he left.'

Lana Parrilla, aka the Evil Queen, was probably closer to the mark. 'I don't know, he may have some bigger opportunities,' she said. 'He may be, you know, doing some huge blockbuster movie in the next few months. He's great and . . . I was so happy when I learned that he got this film because he deserves it and he's . . . I mean, we love Graham, we love Jamie, we miss him on the show, we know he's happy, and he's doing really well, and that warms our hearts.'

The variety of roles being offered to Jamie was testament to his rocketing popularity; now everyone wanted to get him on board their movies. His modelling past was rarely mentioned these days (though Jamie could still be tempted into the odd campaign), as everyone fought to sign up this increasingly hot new star. Even Dakota wasn't receiving the same level of attention: it was Jamie everyone wanted and Jamie who was on everyone's radar.

It wasn't long before another teaser was released, but this one was for *The Fall*. It showed Gillian prone on a bed with Jamie looking menacing in the background. It looked like he'd done for her, but then a few moments later she opened her eyes. Jamie fans might have to wait to see him in *Fifty Shades*, but as a consolation another series of *The Fall* was coming up, which promised plenty of sexual tension between the two lead characters and much speculation about how they might interact.

In the meantime, Jamie's home life continued to be happy. He was loving being a husband and father, and was frequently pictured out with his little family, looking sunny and fresh. He was starting to give back more and more, too, with increasing amounts of charitable work. As well as his father's organization, Tiny Life, he supported Pancreatic Cancer UK, Heartbeat NI and fundraising activities for a young Northern Irish lad named Finton, who collapsed when playing rugby and was subsequently discovered to have cancer. He drew a doodle for the Neurofibromatosis Network, which was auctioned on eBay, and initiatives like these had a real impact, which his fans picked up on, circulating the news more widely.

So what does the future hold? Jamie is clearly poised to become one of the major stars of his generation, the most famous man to emerge from Northern Ireland in years. He has shown that he is more than just a pretty face and that he has substance and range, is able to play vastly different roles and to turn his hand to any number of different projects. In

2014 he gave an interview saying, 'I've done three jobs back to back [*The Fall, New Worlds* and *Fifty Shades*]. Let's see how they are received. If there's nothing I want to do, I'll just play golf and change nappies.' Of course Jamie could afford to do that – and with reports that he had negotiated a percentage of the takings from *Fifty Shades*, the chances are he would end up a seriously rich man – but in actual fact there were no signs of his workload letting up. He knew his time was now and he was going to take advantage of every opportunity as it came along.

'I never felt I was trying to prove anything apart from to myself,' he said in an interview with the *Guardian*. 'But I come at it from a funny angle. Although it looks like I've only been acting a few years, we're talking hundreds and hundreds of failed auditions. I look back on it now and I don't know how anyone gets through the rejection.' He admitted that it was his modelling career that had made it possible for him to keep going. 'I was lucky. If I hadn't been getting paid to model I definitely would have stopped. I would fly off, do a shoot here and there, get paid well, then go back to preparing – and failing – for auditions and meetings.'

It had been a very tough period, but Jamie was aware of the fact that all the rejection had stood him in good stead. An actor can be the most talented in the world, but he or she needs luck to make the final breakthrough and Jamie was aware of that. He wasn't going to let it go to his head and nor was he developing a big ego. He was working hard and making the most of the opportunities that came his way. And so it was that this Belfast boy overcame early tragedy and constant rejection and setbacks, to come through and leapfrog over the biggest acting names of his generation to grab the role everybody wanted. His breakthrough was complete.

When it was announced that Jamie was to play Christian, he made his attitude towards the role clear. 'A lot of people care about this book and I'm not under any illusion that they don't,' he said to *Entertainment Weekly*. 'All I can say is I'm going to do everything in my power to portray Christian Grey as truthfully as possible. I can't guarantee that's going to please everyone – just me being cast doesn't please everyone – but it's happened and I'm going to give it everything.'

It was the same attitude he'd had towards everything he'd set out to achieve so far. He'd come a very long way – and was set to go further still.

Picture Credits

Page 1:   © WENN Ltd/Alamy

Page 2:   Photograph Sipa Press/Jamie Dornan, Eva Mendes,
Kerry Washington, Rose Byrne, Thandie Newton, Carine
Roitfeld and Alexandra Shulman/Rex Features (above);
Jamie Dornan and Eva Mendes, Calvin Klein Jeans
campaign/Charles Guerin/ABACA/PA Images (below)

Page 3:   Jamie Dornan and Mischa Barton/Rex Features (top left);
Photograph by Richard Young/Jamie Dornan and Sienna
Miller/ Rex Features (top right); Jamie Dornan and Keira
Knightley/Getty Images (bottom left); Jamie Dornan and
Keira Knightley/© Jean/EMPICS Entertainment/PA
Images (bottom right)

Page 4:   © AF archive/Alamy (above); Photograph by
Boothnation/Jamie Dornan and Amelia Warner/
Rex Features (below)

Page 5:   Jamie Dornan and Kirsten Dunst in *Marie Antoinette*
(2006)/Capital Pictures (above); Jamie Dornan at the
premiere of *Marie Antoinette*/Getty Images (below)

Page 6:   Photograph by Ophelia Wynne/Camera Press London

Page 7:   Jamie Dornan and Jennifer Morrison in *Once Upon a
Time*/Capital Pictures (above); Jamie Dornan in *Once
Upon a Time*/Capital Pictures (below)

Page 8:   Jamie Dornan in BBC'S *The Fall*, 2003/Allstar Picture
Library (above); Jamie Dornan at the Irish Film and
Television Awards/Getty Images (below)

Page 9:   Jamie Dornan at the *GQ* Awards/PA Images

Page 10: Jamie Dornan in *Fifty Shades of Grey*/Capital Pictures

Page 11: Jamie Dornan and Dakota Johnson in *Fifty Shades of
Grey*/Capital Pictures (above); Jamie Dornan and
Dakota Johnson on set/AKM-GSI (below)

Page 12: Jamie Dornan and Freya Mavor in *New Worlds* (2014)/
Capital Pictures (above); Jamie Dornan on *The Graham
Norton Show* (2014)/Topfoto (below)

Page 13: © Pictorial Press Ltd/Alamy

Page 14: Photograph by Chris O'Donovan

Page 15: Photograph by Ophelia Wynne/Camera Press London

Page 16: Jamie Dornan and Dakota Johnson in *Fifty Shades of
Grey*/Capital Pictures